𒀖𒀖𒀖𒀖𒀖𒀖

# BEYOND THE INHABITED WORLD

𒀖𒀖𒀖𒀖𒀖𒀖

THE MIRROR OF BRITAIN SERIES

*General Editor : Kevin Crossley-Holland*

# BEYOND THE INHABITED WORLD

🔁🔁🔁🔁🔁🔁

## ROMAN BRITAIN

🔁🔁🔁🔁🔁🔁

Anthony Thwaite

ANDRE DEUTSCH

First published 1976 by
André Deutsch Limited
105 Great Russell Street London WC1

Copyright © 1976 by Anthony Thwaite

Printed Offset Litho in Great Britain by
Cox & Wyman Ltd
London, Fakenham and Reading

Colour plates printed by
Raithby Lawrence, Leicester

ISBN 0 233 96790 7

꜅꜅꜅꜅꜅꜅

# ACKNOWLEDGEMENTS

꜅꜅꜅꜅꜅꜅

Acknowledgements are due to the following for permission to reproduce the colour and black and white plates: Aerofilms Limited, 5, 12; Ashmolean Museum, Oxford, 3, 6, 12, 2a, 2b, 2c, 2d, 24, 25, 43, 45 and the coin bearing the head of Constantine on page 55; John Baker, London, from *Roman Roads in Britain* by I. D. Margary, 26; Bodleian Library, Oxford, 13; The Trustees of the British Museum, 14, 4, 7b, 18, 21, 36, 37, 39; Cambridge University Collection, 1, 11, 20, 22, 27, 30; Colchester and Essex Museum, 3, 6, 8, 29; Professor Barry Cunliffe, 15; Department of the Environment, Crown Copyright, 10a, 10b, 11, 44; Leeds City Museum, 5, 7, 8; The London Museum, 1, 9, 10, 16, 28, 40, 41; Norfolk Museums Service, 7a; The Royal Commission on Historical Monuments, 33, 35, and the jet pendant on page 85; The Sussex Archaeological Trust, 2, 13, 14, 17; Warburg Institute, 19, 31, 32, 34a, 34b, 42; The Vindolanda Trust, 23, 38; The Verulamium Museum, St Albans, 4, 9.

Thanks are also due to Ruth Crossley-Holland for her invaluable help with picture research and for drawing the map, and to Robert Eames for his drawings of the Chi-Rho and the Cirencester word square.

⬚⬚⬚⬚⬚⬚

# CONTENTS

⬚⬚⬚⬚⬚⬚

🔲🔲🔲🔲🔲

# PREFACE

🔲🔲🔲🔲🔲

THIS book was written in an attempt to make sense of Roman Britain, by someone who is not a professional archaeologist or historian but who – since the age of seven – has been devoted to the study of the past. It does not pretend to any original research, and I am indebted to the many sources I list in my bibliography. But I have visited all of the major and many of the minor sites mentioned; and I am especially grateful to my daughter Lucy and my godson, Ben Martin, who travelled with me to several of these places. I dedicate the book to them.

ANTHONY THWAITE

# INTRODUCTION

A FEW miles from where I live in Norfolk, a large field stretches away from the road, close to a medieval church. One day in late autumn, when the ground had just been ploughed, I walked across this field; and as I walked, I began to pick up things from the soil – pieces of pottery, bits of glass, tiles. Suddenly I stooped down and picked up a coin. It was about the size of a 2p piece, but much thicker, with an uneven edge. The coin was a dull greenish colour. On one side was a man's head, on the other the figure of a woman holding a shield and a spear.

The things I had found were Roman, because this field, which for centuries has been ploughed and sowed and harvested by farmers, 1,900 years ago was a Roman town, Venta Icenorum. The town walls, made of flint and earth, still surround the field. Once they were 11 feet thick and 20 feet high, and each of the walls had a town gate. Houses and temples and shops and a town hall stood within. There were pottery kilns, workshops for making glass, public baths, and a big market-place in the centre of the town. Nothing is left of these on the surface; but during dry summers, archaeologists have photographed the field from the air and their pictures show the outlines of buildings and streets as crop-marks, like ghostly shapes under the ripening corn (see plate 1).

Venta Icenorum is only one of hundreds of Roman settlements in Britain. There is hardly an area of the British Isles where Roman remains have not been found, from Cornwall to Kent, from west Wales to East Anglia, and even as far north as the

1. Aerial view of Venta Icenorum, Norfolk

extreme tip of Scotland, which the Romans never conquered. For almost 400 years there were Roman troops in Britain: that is as long a period as from the time of Queen Elizabeth I to the present day. And the influence of Roman government and Roman habits lasted much longer than that, among the ordinary people of Britain – those people we call 'Romano-British'.

This book tells you about the life of those people: their houses, farms, shops, temples, roads; how they fitted into the rest of the great Roman Empire, how they were ruled and how they sometimes rebelled against that rule; how they worked, what things they used, what they believed in. We know about these things partly through the remains that have been found in the earth, under modern city streets and almost everywhere where more recent men have disturbed the soil by digging; and partly through the writings of the Romans themselves. Because the Romans were the first people in British history who could write and who left behind them written accounts of their work – and sometimes even of their play.

While I am writing this, I have on the desk next to me that coin I found at Venta Icenorum. Sometimes I pick it up and try to spell out the worn inscription that runs round the edge, surrounding the man's head on one side and the woman with the shield and spear on the other. The man is an Emperor of the first century A.D., the woman is the Roman goddess of Victory.

Whoever dropped that coin one day almost 2,000 years ago was as real as the coin. I try to imagine that person, and the whole distant world of Roman Britain.

᠙᠙᠙᠙᠙᠙

# BEYOND THE INHABITED WORLD

᠙᠙᠙᠙᠙᠙

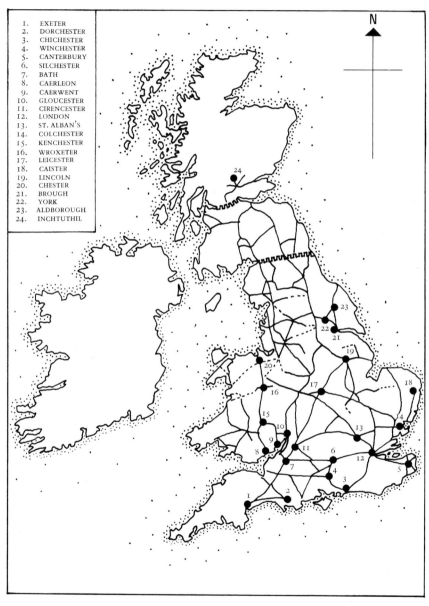

N

Map of Roman Britain showing towns, roads and the two walls.

# THE CONQUEST OF BRITAIN

🔳🔳🔳🔳🔳🔳

ONE of the most famous dates in history is 55 B.C., the year when Julius Caesar made his first invasion of Britain (see plate 2a). He sailed from Gaul (modern France) with his battle fleet, landed on the Kentish coast close to where Deal now stands, and sent about ten thousand soldiers into action. They managed to beat the native Britons after some fierce fighting, but they had advanced only a little way into the country when news came that many of Caesar's ships had been wrecked in a storm: the invasion had taken place late in the year, in September, when the seas were getting rough. So Caesar called back his troops and returned to Gaul, rather than leave them cut off on the enemy island. A year later, in 54 B.C., he tried again, and again made a small advance into Britain, but this time he returned in a hurry because of a revolt that had broken out in Gaul. Although Julius Caesar is always thought of as the great invader of Britain, his invasions were very brief and they achieved very little.

2a. Julius Caesar. After the invasion coins such as the ones shown here and on pages 19, 27, 33, with the heads of the emperors, were in circulation in Britain

But what was the invasion for in the first place? And what sort of country was Caesar invading? You must imagine a land with no roads, hardly anywhere you would call a town, here and there small groups of huts made of stone, turf and earth; dense woods, tangled undergrowth and marsh in much of the lowland country to the south and east, and the hills in these parts crowned by forts ringed with ditches and earth ramparts; a very small, very scattered population, working tiny fields which they ploughed with simple hand-ploughs and whose crops they reaped with iron sickles. They kept cows, sheep, pigs and goats, they made pottery and coins, they were skilful at making beautifully decorated bronze helmets, shields, mirrors and brooches. But these people belonged to separate tribes, which squabbled and fought with one another about the rights of holding land; because over the years the population was growing, new tribes were arriving across the Channel from the east and from Normandy and Brittany, and in those thickly forested plains and valleys good agricultural land was getting scarce.

The Romans had ruled Gaul for a long time; it was one of the richest and most pleasant parts of their Empire, though – as in Britain – the native Gallic tribes still sometimes fought among themselves, and occasionally against the Romans too. Some of these Gauls fled as refugees to Britain; others had come as conquerors themselves. A man called Commius was one of these. Commius had been an ally of Caesar, but when a rival tried to kill him he escaped to Britain, where he managed to set himself up as leader of a tribe called the Atrebates. They settled in Sussex, Hampshire and south Berkshire. It was a war between two other tribes, the Catuvellauni (who lived in a kingdom which stretched from Hertfordshire in the south to the Wash in the east) and the Trinovantes (whose area was Essex and Suffolk), that gave Julius Caesar one of his excuses for invading Britain. Caesar said he was going to make peace between them – which meant that he wanted to conquer both tribes, as well as the tribe of Cantiaci who lived in Kent. Caesar defeated the king of the Catuvellauni near what is now St Albans.

These campaigns of 55–54 B.C. were fierce and bloody for both the Romans and the British tribes. Julius Caesar himself wrote about them, in part of a book called *The Gallic Wars*. He felt that the islands of Britain were a challenge to him; British chiefs had helped those in Gaul to cause trouble to the Romans, and Caesar thought it would be pleasant for the Roman citizens to hear of new victories and conquests on the distant northern edge of the empire, particularly at a time when there was a good deal of political unrest at home. But almost as soon as the king of the Catuvellauni had surrendered, news came from Gaul that that country was getting ready for a new revolt. So Caesar had to hurry back to settle the matter.

The Roman historian, Tacitus, wrote about the period that followed, when in Italy, the heartland of the Empire

> there came the Civil Wars, with the leading men of Rome fighting against their country. Even when peace returned, Britain was long out of mind. Augustus spoke of this as 'policy', Tiberius called it 'precedent'. Gaius Caesar [the Emperor Caligula] unquestionably planned an invasion of Britain; but his quick fancies shifted like a weathercock, and his vast efforts against Germany ended in farce. [Germany was another part of the northern limit of the Empire which the Romans had difficulty in conquering and keeping.] It was Claudius who was responsible for reviving the plan.

The Emperor Claudius (see plate 2b), in fact, was an odd sort of person to plan a victorious campaign. By the time he decided what he wanted to do, almost a century had passed since Julius Caesar's two attempts at invasion. Caligula, about whose German campaigns Tacitus was so rude, had had an ambition to invade Britain, and had even got together an army for this purpose on the coast of Gaul, at Boulogne; but when he ordered his troops

2b. Claudius

down to the seashore, instead of getting them to go on board the ships he told them to pick up seashells. If Caligula was mad (which many people supposed), Claudius seemed little better. He was awkward, inexperienced, physically weak and clumsy, and not at all the kind of leader who inspires confidence. But he knew that to keep his position he had to do something spectacular. Being a Roman ruler was a dangerous and chancy business: Julius Caesar was assassinated, Caligula was murdered. What Claudius decided to do, so that the Romans would admire him, was to conquer Britain – the old dream, discussed so often but put off again and again.

So in A.D. 43 a huge army of about 40,000 men sailed out of the harbour of Boulogne. They landed in the east of Kent, at what is now Richborough, and at first they had difficulty in even finding their enemy. They were probably in rather a gloomy mood anyway: another Roman historian, Dio Cassius, tells how Aulus Plautius, the military commander of the expedition

> had great difficulty in leading his army out of Gaul. The soldiers grumbled at having to campaign beyond the inhabited world (as they put it).

The Romans hated sea journeys, and the soldiers must have loathed the idea of crossing the windy, buffeting Channel to land on an almost unknown island, of which Tacitus wrote: 'The climate is objectionable, with its frequent rains and mists'.

But the Roman leaders knew that it was a good moment to invade. King Cunobelinus, who had extended the power of the Catuvellauni well beyond the bounds of his predecessors, had died a year or so earlier, and the tribal area had been split between two of his sons, Togodumnus and Caratacus. In the dispute over who was to rule what, another son, Adminius, had fled to the Romans, so loyalties were divided. In Sussex, part of the old kingdom of the Atrebates which Commius had once ruled was in the hands of a tribal king called Verica, who somehow became a refugee at the court of Claudius in Rome. So part of the invasion zone was weakened by quarrels between new rulers, and part was probably ready to surrender because the ruler had already gone over to the Roman enemy.

You can imagine the four Legions of the invading Roman army making their way suspiciously from Richborough through the woods of Kent, wondering when they were actually going to see their enemy. They had expected strong resistance on the coast, even if their generals imagined that the Catuvellauni and the Atrebates were going to be easily conquered eventually. But there was no resistance. It was uncanny.

What had happened was that the British had heard from friends in Gaul of the trouble Aulus Plautius was having in persuading his troops to embark. The British warriors had got restless (because they were not full-time soldiers on the whole, but chiefly farmers who did some military service when it was necessary), and had gone home. They had heard so many rumours of a Roman invasion in the past, and now it seemed that the news was just another rumour. So the Legions got all the way to the River Medway, in northern Kent, before there was any sign of anyone trying to stop them. Then, probably at a crossing-point of the river just above what is now Rochester, they found the British, hurriedly brought together again, waiting for them on the other side.

What the British did not know was that a river crossing was a quite different thing for the Roman troops from crossing the Channel: Roman soldiers might grumble about sailing across the sea, but they were well trained to cross rivers. Special groups of them were very skilful at swimming while wearing their full equipment. They made a surprise attack, swarmed on to the opposite bank, and immediately began hurling their javelins, not at the British, but at the horses that pulled the British war chariots. So the charioteers were in confusion, and a second wave of Roman troops (headed by Vespasian, who was later to become Emperor himself) crossed the river and slaughtered large numbers of both charioteers and foot soldiers. The next day the British briefly rallied, but they could not resist the wave after wave of Romans who crossed the river. The strongest British tribe in the south was beaten.

This was perhaps the most important battle fought on British soil until William the Conqueror's victory near Hastings in 1066. Although there were more battles for the Romans to fight, and although they never succeeded in totally putting the whole of the British Isles under their rule, this battle on the Medway meant that the disunited British tribes were unlikely to put up any kind of struggle with which the Roman Legions could not cope. The Romans were highly trained, well-experienced, well-equipped. There were still fierce tribes in Wales, in Yorkshire, in Scotland; but the southern and eastern lowlands of Britain were to fall comparatively easily.

It was at this moment, with the victory on the Medway, that Aulus Plautius apparently realised that he would have little trouble in reaching and occupying the chief enemy capital of the region, Camulodunum; and because the decision to invade Britain had been made by Claudius, it was the duty of the general to tell his Emperor what was about to happen. Indeed, only the Emperor should lead his victorious troops into the conquered capital.

Camulodunum lies underneath what is now the town of Colchester in Essex. We know very little about what it looked like when it was the capital of the Catuvellauni; although the tribe was a rich and powerful one, the town itself was probably an unimpressive collection of huts. But for Claudius, hurrying through Gaul from Rome to his triumphant reception in the newly conquered island, it was to be the chief city of Britain. Inscriptions found there show that its official Roman name became *Colonia Claudia Victricensis* – the colony of Claudius the Victorious. A colonia, or colony, was the Roman name for a settlement of soldiers retired from the regular army; the idea was that these people would be useful in keeping the place safe for the Romans, and that they would show the native people how to lead the Roman way of life. And one of the first buildings the Romans made to show this way of life was a great stone temple, the oldest stone and mortar building in Britain (see plate 3), dedicated to the Emperor Claudius himself – because the Romans considered the Emperor, even when he was as feeble-looking as Claudius, to be

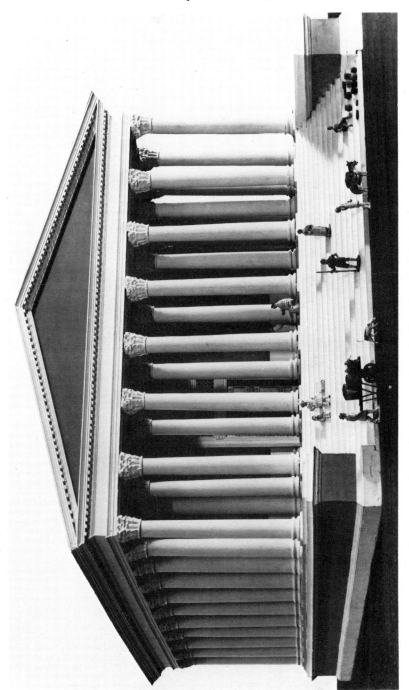

3. Reconstruction of the temple of Claudius in Colchester Museum

a god. The huge bronze head of Claudius found at Colchester probably came from this temple (see plate 4).

4. Bronze head of the Emperor Claudius found at Colchester

Claudius was in Britain for only sixteen days. By the time he returned to Rome, after having accepted the surrender of eleven British kings, his orders were clear to Aulus Plautius and the other Roman generals: they were 'to subjugate the remaining districts'. This was the job that occupied them for the next few years. One Legion pushed west as far as Dorset; two others went into the Midlands, establishing a frontier zone along which the great Roman road, the Fosse Way, was soon to run diagonally across England; and a fourth moved north to Lincoln.

Some of this military movement naturally met resistance, especially from the tribe of Durotriges, who lived in what is now Dorset. Modern excavations at some of the hill-forts of the Durotriges have shown evidence of fierce fighting as the Romans attacked. Near Dorchester, for example, the Second Legion seem to have captured Maiden Castle (see plate 5) without using any of their siege-engines or stone-throwing slings; but the skeletons of the defenders of this great earth castle fortified with ramparts and ditches show the deep sword cuts which had sliced into them. One British skeleton grimly contains the head of a Roman ballista (a heavy iron bolt fired from a mechanical bow), which entered the body in the chest, broke through a bone in the spine, and thrust part-way through the back. At Hod Hill, another hill-fort eighteen miles north of Maiden Castle, a whole pile of ballista heads was found round a large hut, as if the Roman soldiers had particularly concentrated on killing or capturing one of the chieftains.

Caratacus had fled after the battle on the Medway to south Wales, and led resistance from there. He was later captured and taken in triumph to Rome. North of Lincoln lived the fierce tribe of the Brigantes, and it took another thirty years for the Romans to push firmly into this territory and found the fort and town of Eboracum (later York). Even the lowland areas, which at first had collapsed so easily to the Romans, sometimes caused trouble in these early years of occupation. In the year 60 A.D., while the chief Roman troops were busy trying to subdue Wales, Boudicca, the Queen of a small tribe (the Iceni) in what is now Norfolk took this chance to raise a rebellion (Boudicca is popularly

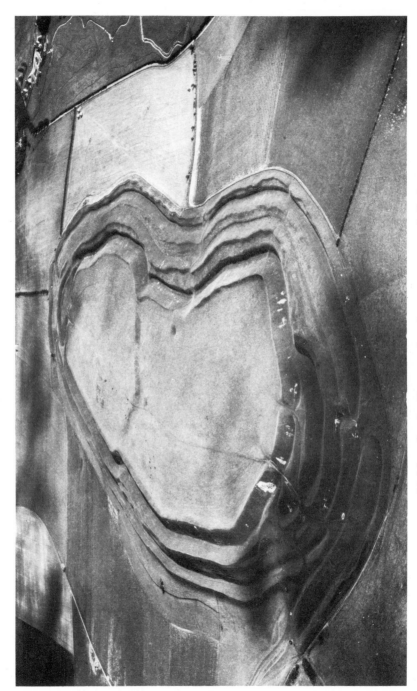

5.  Maiden Castle, Dorset, showing ramparts and ditches

known as Boadicea). Camulodunum was attacked and most of its buildings, including the great temple of Claudius, were burnt to the ground.

A number of the Trinovantes joined with their old tribal enemies, the Iceni, against the hated Roman oppressor who was taxing them so heavily, who had tried to confiscate their weapons, had robbed them of so much land, and who had executed or exiled their chieftains. One picture will give a good idea of what the British felt about the occupying army: the tombstone of a Roman cavalry officer, who died before the rebellion and who was buried at Colchester. This man, Longinus, came from the eastern part of the Roman Empire, in what is now Bulgaria. On his monument is carved the figure of himself on horseback, triumphantly crushing a British warrior who is cowering under the horse's hooves. The Briton is made to look more like a hairy animal than a man. When Boudicca's rebels reached Camulodunum, they smashed Longinus's tombstone in two, and deliberately destroyed the proud face of the man on horseback (see plate 6).

After the destruction of Camulodunum, Boudicca's army pressed on to the old capital of the Catuvellauni, Verulamium (now St Albans), which the Romans had made into an important town, and to the newly founded trading port on the river Thames, Londinium (London). They destroyed both places. Londinium had already become the financial capital of the Roman province of Britannia, and was the headquarters of probably the most hated Roman official of all – Catus Decianus. This man had been sent to Britain by the Emperor to be in charge of all tax-gathering. The army campaigns and the administration of the new province, with the construction of many buildings and roads, was an expensive business – so expensive that the Emperor Nero (see plate 2c), who had succeeded Claudius, at one point almost

2c. Nero

6. The tomb of Longinus smashed by Boudicca's rebels

decided to give up and withdraw all his troops. But Catus
Decianus had been particularly successful in ruthlessly getting
money from the British, and the Romans stayed on. However, he
was so terrified by Boudicca's attack that as her rebels reached
Londinium, he rapidly packed his bags, summoned his staff, and
fled by boat back to Gaul.

But Boudicca's army, though large, was not well disciplined,
and the highly trained Romans were bound to win in the end. The
military governor, Suetonius, who had followed on after Aulus
Plautius's retirement, hurried back from Wales. At some point
which has not yet been identified, the two armies met at the mouth
of a narrow valley. In the battle that followed, the Romans
claimed that 80,000 Britons were killed, and only 400 Romans.
Boudicca poisoned herself before she could be captured. The
Roman revenge afterwards was terrible. But at this point the
new financial officer, Classicianus, who had replaced the greedy
and cowardly Catus Decianus, decided that things could not go on
like this: otherwise the province of Britannia would be ruined and
no one would benefit. So he wrote to the Emperor Nero, advising
him that a new military governor should be sent over: if Suetonius
remained, he would go on killing and destroying, and a proper
peace would never be made.

The new governors, each of whom stayed in the job between
three and six years, were determined to keep the peace in most of
Britain while extending the frontiers north and west. The most
famous of them was Agricola, who was governor from A.D. 78 to 85:
we probably know most about him because it happened that the
historian Tacitus married his daughter, and in fact wrote a whole
book about his father-in-law. One of the first things Agricola did
when he arrived in Britain was to conquer the island of Anglesey,
off the north coast of Wales, which was the stronghold of the
Druids, the fierce priests of the Britons. After that, he decided
(in Tacitus's words) 'to root out the causes of war'. He made wise
appointments among officials who were to work under him,
making sure they were honest. He saw that justice was properly
carried out. He gave orders that the compulsory 'gifts' of corn
and other goods which the conquered tribes had to hand over to

the Romans were fairly organised, and reduced some of the taxes which the British most disliked. So (says Tacitus) 'Agricola gave men reason to love and honour peace'.

The result was that the tribes of the midlands, the east, the south-east and the south-west became a peaceful part of the Roman Empire, almost without interruption, for over 300 years, until the invasions and other troubles which the last chapter of this book deals with. During this long peaceful period, a remarkable new civilization grew up from the south coast to the far north of Yorkshire, and from the Welsh border to the coast of Boudicca's old kingdom in the east. A Roman military government still continued to rule, and from time to time to campaign, in parts of Wales, parts of the north, and in Scotland. But most of the rest of this story is of ordinary life, not of war.

1. Reconstruction of Roman London, A.D. 200

2. Gilded bronze head of the goddess Minerva, from Bath

3. Ceiling plaster from Verulamium

4. Lion mosaic from Verulamium

㽝㽝㽝㽝㽝㽝

# LIFE IN THE TOWNS

㽝㽝㽝㽝㽝㽝

VENTA ICENORUM, the place in Norfolk which I wrote about in my Introduction, and where I found the Roman coin, is a good example of a small town in Roman Britain. The name means, in Latin, 'the market-place of the Iceni' – and this was the very area from which Queen Boudicca and her rebel tribe of Iceni came. But this town began to be built by the Romans a few years after the rebellion, in what was probably a deliberate attempt to get the British to settle down peacefully. The town became, in fact, the administrative capital of the old tribal area. From all the bits of evidence used by archaeologists (air photographs, excavations which show foundations of buildings, the pottery and coins and glass and metal objects which lie under the surface and on top of it), we can get a picture of what kind of life the Romans led in towns.

The first thing to remember is that very few of these 'Romans' were from Rome, or Italy, at all. When the town was first founded, in about the year A.D. 70, a few of the chief local government officials and planners must have been Roman citizens, and they would have tried to get the co-operation of whoever was left among the leading families of the Iceni after the slaughter and executions for which Suetonius was responsible after Boudicca's defeat. But even these Roman citizens were not necessarily from Rome itself. The Roman Empire stretched from Babylon to Morocco, from Spain to Turkey, from Austria to Egypt; and

Roman armies and officials came from all these places, and everywhere in between. If you look at the four Legions that formed the invading army of Aulus Plautius in A.D. 43, you get some idea of how many different kinds of people were contained in the Empire. One Legion came from France, two from Germany, one from Hungary. Added to these were auxiliary troops from Holland. A little later, auxiliary troops came to Britain from Spain, Morocco, Rumania and Syria. (See plates 7a and 7b.)

7a. A cavalry helmet from Norfolk

In the same way, government officials, architects, craftsmen and merchants in the province of Britain came from many parts of the Roman Empire. As the years went by, some of these – as well

7b. Legionary's helmet from London

as the soldiers – married local girls; and so, as generation followed generation, a mixed population grew. All spoke some Latin, the official language of the Empire, but they would probably do so with their local accents, and at home they would speak their own language – in Venta, it was a kind of Celtic. It was said of a later Emperor, Septimius Severus (see plate 2d), that for the whole of his life he spoke Latin with his native North African accent, because he was born and brought up in the city of Leptis Magna, in what is now Libya.

2d. Septimius Severus

The mixed population which gradually inhabited the province of Britannia we call 'Romano-British'. To begin with, the inhabitants of Venta Icenorum were probably a little uneasy about being organized in Roman fashion, but after all they had their livings to earn: farmers wanted to sell their produce and cattle, shopkeepers and stall holders in the market looked for customers. At this time, towards the end of the first century A.D., the town was a collection of small flimsy huts, no different from the kind they had lived in before the Romans came. No traces have been found of any public buildings in Venta dating from this period. The main difference between this new town and the tiny settlements that preceded it was that the streets at Venta were laid out at regular right angles, without going higgledy-piggledy all over the place. This was the usual pattern of all Roman towns, big and small, and it was a pattern that the Romans had learnt from the Greeks. Round the town were built defensive walls (see plate 8).

Another difference was that a proper road was built from Camulodunum to Venta, with small villages and inns along it where horses could be changed and where travellers could rest on their journey; and wooden bridges were built over the rivers on the way. Throughout the Roman Empire, roads were the most important – and often the first – pieces of construction. In such a highly organized society as the Empire, it was necessary for officials and military commanders to be closely in touch with what was going on everywhere. Until the Romans came, the only means of communication were rough trackways.

Within about thirty years (that is, soon after A.D. 100), the first public buildings were erected at Venta. A forum was laid out in the centre of the town, which was used for public meetings and as a market-place. Facing on to the forum was the basilica, or town hall, where the chief citizens of Venta would meet to discuss the governing of the place, and where the law courts could be found. To the west, down near the river, public baths were built, and the water supply came from the river through wooden pipes. Small factories began to develop, including a group of kilns for making pottery. With this new prosperity the design of the houses improved, so that they were no longer huts but more solid buildings: some of them had their own small bath-houses.

The defensive ditches that run all round the town, some of which can still clearly be seen today, were dug at this time, though

8. Roman town wall, Balkerne Hill, Colchester

it was another hundred years before the town walls were built. Then two temples were built near the forum, though we cannot tell which gods were worshipped in them. Perhaps one of them was for 'the deified emperors' – that is, all those emperors from Augustus onwards who were given the rank of gods; and perhaps the other was for some local god or gods of the Iceni, because the Romans on the whole were quite tolerant in allowing their widely scattered subjects to follow whatever religion seemed to be native to the place – as long as the people behaved properly like good Romans, obeyed the laws, and paid their taxes.

Workshops for the manufacture of glass developed at Venta later (see plate 9). Only two other places in Roman Britain are known to have made glass (Colchester and Warrington). The Romans used window-glass, and they also made glass into large

9. Examples of Roman glasswork

sealed jars, in which the cremated remains of the dead were placed for burial. The most elaborately decorated glass, made into vases and bowls, came from glass factories in Egypt and Syria.

Venta was always only a small town, and in any case it is perhaps difficult now to imagine what it looked like and what life there was like, because so little is left of it on the surface. We get a clearer picture of it by studying the reports of excavations made there in the 1920s and 1930s and by seeing the things they found which are now displayed in Norwich Castle Museum. Most of these things are of course the objects the people used in their everyday lives. There is pottery, both the rather rough greyish-black kind that was made on the spot in the Venta kilns and which was the ordinary kitchen stuff, and pots that were brought in by merchants from other places – including the shiny red kind, with moulded decorations, which is usually called Samian ware and which was made in Gaul. There are roof tiles, floor tiles, bricks (some of these were re-used in the Middle Ages when the church was being built), and bits of square coloured stone called tesserae which were laid out in patterns to make mosaic floors. There are tools (see plate 10) – parts of sickles; knives, meat cleavers and meat hooks from butchers' shops; parts of shopkeepers' weighing scales. There are brooches, used for fastening the clothes (before buttons and zips), most of which are like fancy versions of safety-pins. There are hardly any weapons, because Venta was not a military place, and for several hundred years it must have been peaceful. And there are coins, mostly made of bronze, but some silver ones, and even a very few gold, such as a coin of the Emperor Nero (see plate 2c).

Venta is one of the few Roman towns in Britain which has not been built over in later times: the fact that we can see so little of it today is due, not to other buildings sitting on top of it, but to the amount of ready-made stone that the medieval inhabitants of the area carted off and used for buildings elsewhere. It became the tiny village of Caistor St Edmund. An old Norfolk rhyme says:

> Caistor was a city when Norwich was none,
> and Norwich was built with Caistor stone.

Norwich is only a few miles down the road, and we can imagine that the masons who built that city's great medieval churches were very glad to find such a good supply of already prepared material almost on their doorstep. And when the Roman buildings had been pulled down to their foundations, the farmers came in and ploughed the land where they stood, turning them into fields, which they have been from that day to this.

10 (left and above). Roman tools for use in the kitchen, on the farm and in shops

Another Roman town – much bigger than Venta – which has never been built over is Silchester, near Reading. It was called by the Romans Calleva Atrebatum – Calleva of the tribe of Atrebates; so it was originally the capital of the northern part of that tribe which was ruled for a time by Verica, the traitor chieftain I mentioned in Chapter One. Nowadays Silchester is a large (120 acres) area of ploughland, with no remains of buildings above the ground; but all round it are the Roman walls of the town, surrounded by a massive bank and ditch. These walls are made of lumps of flint bonded with mortar to blocks of limestone, and they stand up tall and strong among the fields (see plate 11) – though all they surround now are the crops of farmers, who don't need such defences.

11. Aerial view of Silchester, Hampshire

If you look at a map of Roman Britain (see map on page 16), you will see that most of the towns the Romans built are still inhabited, beginning with some of the earliest: Camulodunum became Colchester, Verulamium became St Albans (though the Roman town lay a little outside the later city), Londinium became London. Of these, Londinium had become the capital of the whole province of Britannia by the end of the first century A.D. (see colour plate 1). Verulamium was a municipium – that is, a town which was given its own rights and privileges by order of the Emperor. Camulodunum, built specially for retired soldiers as a colonia, was one of four such towns, the other three being Eboracum (York), Lindum (Lincoln) and Glevum (Gloucester). Apart from Venta Icenorum and Calleva Atrebatum, there were many other 'tribal capitals', such as Ratae Coritanorum (Leicester), Viroconium Cornoviorum (Wroxeter), Venta Silurum (Caerwent, in Monmouthshire), Venta Belgarum (Winchester), and Durovernum Cantiacorum (Canterbury). Some towns were chiefly army fortresses, round which settlements of traders and suchlike grew; Deva Victrix (Chester) was one of these. And one town came into being because its springs of warm water were considered to be both sacred and good for the health: this was Aquae Sulis (Bath).

What all these towns basically had in common was a layout that hardly varied throughout the whole Roman world. As at Venta Icenorum (see plate 1) streets ran straight and crossed at right-angles. There was a main road running north and south, known as the cardo, and another main road running east and west, known as the decumanus. These main roads linked the four gates of the town. Somewhere at the centre was the forum, the main square, with the basilica at one end. Behind each block formed by the intersection of the streets lay the shops and houses. These features can be found in the capital of the Empire itself, Rome, as well as in all the scattered provinces, from Palmyra in Syria to Cordoba in Spain, from Leptis Magna in North Africa to Trier in Germany, and throughout the settled part of Britain.

This uniformity of the Roman town plan was part of a uniformity which the Romans brought to all kinds of activity:

laws, language, bathing and sanitation, weights and measures, military equipment, costume, heating, schooling, even public pleasures such as the events that went on in their theatres and amphitheatres. Several places in Roman Britain had simple wooden amphitheatres, which would be used for animal baiting (of bulls and bears) and for wrestling and fights between gladiators. Remains of them have been found at Chester and at Caerleon in Wales, for instance. The best visible example in Britain of a true Roman theatre, with its stage and its semi-circle of stone seats, is at St Albans (see plate 12). Close by there was a temple and a sacred enclosure, because for the Romans (as for the Greeks) theatres were places for religious festivals as well as for ordinary entertainments.

It must have been bewildering for the British tribes to have all these complicated matters of town life thrust on them within a short space of time. The small straggling settlements, the isolated farms, the hill-forts for temporary refuge during periods of tribal warfare – all these disappeared in the lowland parts of Britain as the Romans extended their roads, their military bases and their towns. The very way in which these towns were administered was characteristically Roman. Although the Roman administration throughout the Empire was usually quite tolerant about accepting any kind of local tribal organization which they happened to find in a new province (just as they were tolerant of local religions), the possibility of another native rising like Boudicca's probably meant that the standard Roman pattern of local government was made compulsory.

We know from inscriptions (found at Bath, Lincoln and York) that local government officials called decurions were elected. Some of these would have been retired army officers and other full Roman citizens, but in the early days of the Roman province some of them must have been members of the native tribal aristocracy – chieftains or sons of chieftains who were willing to co-operate with the new rulers. Together the decurions made up the ordo, or local senate. They were responsible for seeing that the taxes were collected efficiently, and every year four of them were

12. The Roman theatre at St Albans

specially elected to be magistrates: two of them were picked to act as judges of law cases (though the most important cases would have to be sent to the Roman governor), and two were appointed to supervise such jobs as the construction of public buildings, the making and maintenance of roads, drainage, public baths, and so on. It was an expensive business to be a decurion, because they were expected to pay substantial contributions to help with all the money necessary for such things.

So gradually the Roman way of life was taken up in all these towns of Roman Britain. Tacitus wrote about the governor, Agricola, like this:

> To persuade a people, until now scattered, uncivilised and therefore likely to fight, to grow pleasurably used to peace and ease, Agricola gave private encouragement and official assistance to the building of temples, public squares and private mansions. He trained the sons of the chiefs in the arts of civilisation. . . . The result was that in place of dislike for the Latin language there came a passion to be skilful in it. In the same way, our national dress came into favour and the toga was everywhere to be seen. And so the Britons were gradually led on to the luxuries that make vice pleasant – arcades, baths, and splendid banquets. They spoke of such novelties as 'civilisation', when really they were only a form of enslavement.

Of course Tacitus is here mocking the British, in a rather superior way, for enthusiastically taking up the softer side of Roman life: it is like a modern journalist laughing at, say, newly rich Arabs for buying big Cadillacs. But the serious point is that it shows how, as early as the end of the first century A.D., town life was developing quickly in Britain because the British wanted it.

If the forum and the basilica were the most important public parts of a Roman town, the public baths were not far behind them. Every town of any size had them, and often more than one set. Going to the baths was not just a matter of keeping clean: they were places where you went to meet your friends, to gossip, to play – and, in chilly Britain, no doubt a place where you went to get warm if you were not fortunate enough to have central heating in your house. Most public baths were built next to the palaestra, a sports ground where people could run races, play games, or wrestle. Within the baths themselves, the same series of rooms can be found – with small variations – all over the Roman Empire. At Silchester, for example, there was first a courtyard inside the entrance, with a colonnaded walk round it. On the far side of the courtyard was the apodyteria, or changing room, where you undressed and went into the frigidarium, a room with a cold plunge-bath in it; then to a slightly warmer room, the tepidarium (in some public baths the order of these rooms was reversed), before going into the really hot room, the caldarium. It was here, or in rooms off it, that the masseurs and manicurists worked, rubbing oil into customers' bodies, massaging and pummelling them, scraping them with a scraper known as a strigil (which removed the oil and sweat), plucking out body hair, and no doubt chatting away at the hot and exhausted people who were in their hands.

Then you would probably return the way you came, finally having a cold plunge to accustom you to the temperature of the outside world. Seneca, the Roman philosopher and playwright, actually lived above a public bath-house in Rome; and at about the time the first public baths were being built in the new province of Britannia, he wrote an amusing account of the sounds he heard:

> Imagine all the noises that offend my ears! When a strenuous man is exercising himself by lifting lead weights, for example – when he is working hard (or pretending to work hard) I can hear him grunt; and when he releases his breath after holding it, I can hear him panting and wheezing. Or there is a lazy man, who is just content with being massaged with oil – I can hear the blows of the masseur's hand on his shoulder, varying in tone according to whether the hand is laid on flat or hollow. Someone begins to throw up a ball and counts the number of times he catches it . . . Sometimes I hear a drunk or a pickpocket being arrested, and the noise of someone in the bath who loves to hear his own voice, or the keen fellow who plunges into the

pool with tremendous splashing . . . And there's the manicurist, with his shrill voice – the only time he's quiet is when he's plucking hairs from someone's armpits, and then the customer is screaming in pain . . . On top of all that, there are the cries of the sausage-man, the cake-seller, and all the other men selling food. Each of them has his own special tone of voice.

The biggest and most famous baths in Britain were at Bath itself, which from an early stage in the Roman occupation specialized in making use of the local hot springs and the healing mineral waters (see plate 13). The Roman name of Bath, Aquae Sulis, means 'the waters of Sulis' – Sulis was a local god of the area. Statues and inscriptions have been found in Bath which seem to show that the particular local goddess of Roman times

13. Part of the Great Bath at Bath, with masonry from the vault lying in the centre

5. Romulus and Remus mosaic found at Aldborough, North Yorkshire

6. Roman writing materials and lamp from Verulamium

7. Model of Fishbourne Palace about 75 A.D.

8. Dolphin mosaic from Fishbourne

was Sulis Minerva – and Minerva was the Roman goddess of healing, among other things (see colour plate 2). The temple of Sulis Minerva lay very close to the baths themselves, which were rebuilt and extended several times during the Roman period. Part of the waters of the main spring were even led into a corner of the temple grounds, where they were held in a big lead-lined tank. This reservoir was a sacred place: when it was excavated in modern times, the bottom of the tank was covered with all kinds of offerings that people had made, perhaps when asking help of the goddess in an illness or thanking her for a cure. There were coins, brooches, dice, a pin decorated with a pearl, a gold earring, a bag of 33 engraved gem stones, and even a tin mask. The oddest thing of all was a small lead sheet, on which somebody had scratched a curse: each word is written backwards, as if in code so that only the goddess could understand it, and the translation reads:

> May he who carried off Vilbia from me become as liquid as water.
> May he who wickedly devoured her become dumb, whether it is . . .

and there then follows a list of nine names, one of whom the writer suspected was the culprit (see plate 14).

The whole business of an efficient water supply was very important to the Romans, not only for baths but also for drinking and drainage. Most places depended on wells, lined with timber and rubble; occasionally (as at Silchester) old wooden barrels with their bottoms knocked out were used for these linings. But sometimes the wells could not supply enough water, and aqueducts had to be built – long lengths of pipe, sometimes raised above the ground, sometimes running under it, which brought water from some pool, spring or stream, and which in at least one case (at Lincoln) needed to have a force-pump attached with which to lift the water into a reservoir. Whenever possible, the waste water from public fountains and baths was used to flush out the drainage and sewage channels.

Before the Roman occupation and the beginning of town life, the British tribes had relied on providing food for themselves, weaving their own clothes and making their own pottery, and had

14. Curse scratched on a sheet of lead found in the reservoir, Bath

turned to travelling merchants (some from Gaul, some local) only for such special things as certain tools, weapons, and luxuries like jewellery and ornaments. But very soon after the arrival of the Romans, shops began to spring up in the new towns. At Verulamium, archaeologists excavated a row of wooden shops which had been built within a few years of the invasion in A.D. 43. Each consisted of a room measuring about 16 feet by 20 feet, with a slightly smaller room behind. The shops were arranged in blocks of four: in front of them was a colonnade, with wooden columns supporting a sloping roof, so that the pedestrians had a covered walk against the rain. The front rooms of the shops opened straight on to the street, so that the counters would be laid out right under the customers' noses. In the front part of one shop two bronze-working places were found; the owners were probably engravers or grinders. But these shops in Verulamium have not revealed as much as they might otherwise have done, because they were burned down by Boudicca's rebels in A.D. 60.

Indeed, even in peacetime fire was one of the chief dangers in a Roman town. Although from the beginning the important public buildings, such as the basilica, the temples and the baths, were built of stone (and, after a time, the private houses of the better-off citizens), there were always a number of timber houses and shops, and once a fire had started it was difficult to stop. Many Roman towns show signs of both large fires and small ones. Sometimes it was several years before rebuilding was completed after these fires, presumably because there was difficulty in raising money. In A.D. 155, a fire at Verulamium destroyed over 50 acres of the city.

Even without fires, life in the towns could have other public problems. For example, street repairs caused trouble. Streets, other than the main highways, were made of packed gravel or rubble, and when they had to be repaired the method was simply to put a new layer of gravel on top of the old. These 'repairs' have been measured at Cirencester (which the Romans called Corinium), and the measurements have shown that over a period of 350 years the street surface rose as much as three feet. In dry weather the dust would blow into the shopfronts and housefronts, but – much worse – in wet weather the mud would wash into front rooms. So the wretched shopkeeper or householder would in the end decide to pull down his building, level off the site, and rebuild it so that it stood at least a little way above the street, not below it. This is partly why archaeologists find so many levels of occupation when they are excavating a Roman town.

But if street life could be unpleasant, the Romans put a great deal of effort into making their houses as comfortable as possible, in Britain as in all the settled parts of the Roman Empire. In the next chapter I shall give details about the typical house in the country, usually called a 'villa'. One of the main differences between town houses and country houses was that in the town they were quite often two storeys high. The walls of the ground floor were built of local stone, or sometimes brick: the upper part of a mixture of clay and straw ('wattle and daub') packed in between a timber framework. Inside, the lower walls were covered with stucco or plaster, which was painted, sometimes in plain colours, sometimes with decorations or even pictures. In Britain, most of these coloured plaster walls can be seen only in fragments (see colour plate 3), but at Pompeii in Italy many of them are complete.

Sometimes the town houses were L-shaped, sometimes they were built round a central courtyard or quadrangle, where there were bushes, flower-beds and, in the richer houses, a fountain and statues. The main entrance was a large gateway, up to 10 feet wide, with large wooden double doors. A corridor would run towards the rooms themselves, which led out of each other, from living-room to dining-room and on to bedrooms, kitchen quarters, rooms for servants, and perhaps a garden or orchard beyond – these were fairly common at Silchester and Caerwent.

Because they were made of material that does not easily survive, such as wood, a great deal of the furniture and furnishings of Romano-British houses is known to us only through fragments, or through the occasional carvings or paintings of these things that have been found. But fortunately the Romans were fond of an art that has managed to last much longer because the material used was stone: I mean mosaic, and especially mosaic pavements. Apart from the many examples from villas, which I shall come to later, mosaic pavements from town houses have been found at Verulamium (see colour plate 4), Silchester, London, Cirencester, and several other places. The pavements from Cirencester are particularly fine: it was a prosperous country town, made rich by its manufacture of wool, and the inhabitants were able to support a firm of mosaic workers which centred on the place. This firm had its own little tricks of style, which can be recognized in over 40 pavements in Cirencester and close by. It is amazing what vivid pictures could be created from these small cubes and chips of coloured stone, the tesserae. The Romans were so fond of this art that they would go to enormous pains to employ the best craftsmen: those from North Africa, particularly from what is now Tunisia and eastern Algeria, were the most highly thought of, and it may even be that some of the earlier Romano-British examples were made, or at least designed, by these Africans.

Scenes from mythology were favourite subjects for mosaics, as they were for much Roman art. One from Cirencester shows Orpheus playing his lute to the animals: Orpheus is sitting on a rock, with his dog beside him. A common type showed pictures of the Four Seasons, or the Nine Muses of the arts. Animals, birds and fish were much liked – deer, dogs, dolphins, and (from a pavement in Leicester) a large peacock. At Aldborough (Yorkshire), which was the most northern town in Roman Britain, a pavement was found which shows one of the basic Roman subjects, pictured over and over again in carvings, on coins, and elsewhere – the story of Romulus and Remus, the legendary founders of Rome itself, looked after by a wolf when they were abandoned as babies. In the Aldborough pavement, the wolf is grinning and showing her big teeth; she stands with one paw raised, while the two babies seem to be dancing about (see colour plate 5). All these pavements were regarded as very precious: at Lisbon, in Portugal, a mosaic pavement was found which had some warning words in Latin set into the design, obviously intended for servants – 'Don't hurt the mosaic with a scratchy broom, be careful of it'.

Public buildings and the better houses had windows fitted with small panes of glass (usually greenish and not very clear by our standards), but at night there was no public lighting in the streets, and the rooms of all types of building were lit by candles or by lamps burning olive oil. Some of these lamps were made of metal and had several wicks, which would have given a fairly good light, but most of them were small, made of pottery, held only a little oil, and had only a single wick (see colour plate 6). If you went out at night, you would probably carry a torch made out of rushes and dipped in pitch, which gave a flaring, smoky sort of light. Most people went to bed early and got up early, at dawn or before.

Still, if the inhabitants of Roman towns had only dim lighting, they were no worse off in this than the inhabitants of Britain for many centuries to come, right down to the invention of gas lights and, later, electric lights in the nineteenth century; and many of them were considerably better off when it came to heating their houses. They had the most efficient form of central heating in existence until the present day. What is known as the hypocaust

15. Hypocaust

system involved building raised floors supported on pillars, so that hot air could circulate under the rooms (see plate 15). The hot air was made by a furnace built outside the house, which was stoked with wood (and sometimes coal) by the house servants. The air then flowed through channels through the foundations, and was eventually carried away through hollow tiles built into the walls of the rooms, and out into the open: as the air travelled through the tiles it heated the walls as well. All this could only be done, of course, in houses which were solidly built of stone or brick: the floors themselves had to be made of stone or mosaic rather than wood. Even so, the system was probably no more dangerous than, say, modern portable oil heaters, and it gave a more evenly distributed heat. More elaborate versions of these hypocausts were used in the public baths, where they were adapted to heat the water as well. Modern experiments have been made to see how much effort was needed to keep a Roman house warm in this way, and they have shown that an average-sized room (17 feet by 15 feet) took a day and a half for the floor to get properly hot; but after that it could be kept at an even temperature of just over 70 degrees fahrenheit with the furnace being stoked only twice a day – rather like a modern solid-fuel domestic boiler. In really cold weather, when the people in the house wanted to increase the temperature, they had to wear thick-soled shoes or sandals to protect their feet from the hot floors (see plate 16).

Visitors to towns, such as travellers on business and officials, would need to stay in inns or hotels, and to eat and drink in restaurants and wine shops. The best preserved examples of these in the Roman Empire can be found in Italy, especially in the ruins of Pompeii, Herculaneum (both of these near Naples), and Ostia, the port of Rome. An example of an inn at Pompeii has a large dining-room, and opening off it six bedrooms and a kitchen. Some of the guests had scratched their names on the bedroom walls – two friends, Lucius and Primigenius, sharing one room, and four actors in another. Another scratched inscription says that Eupor had a party at the inn with nineteen friends.

16. Roman sandals

In Britain there are no remains of inns as vivid as this. The best one was found at Silchester, where a big building just inside the south gate of the town has corridors of apartments round a court-yard, a large series of baths, and a building attached which may have been a stable and wagon shed, where horses could be kept for when the traveller moved on again. Near the south gate of Caerwent, too, there is a similar large house with over forty rooms, and at the port of Caister-by-Yarmouth, on the coast of Norfolk, another large building is thought to have been a hostel for seamen staying there until they caught their next ship.

Outside the gates by which the inns at Silchester and Caerwent were built, the roads led away to the next towns; and not far from the gates and walls, and always outside them, were the cemeteries. By Roman law, the dead were not allowed to be buried within the town. But the ceremonies for the dead, and what the people of Roman Britain believed about the spirits of the dead and the living, must wait for a later chapter. Before that, we must look at how people lived away from the towns, on the villas and farms scattered across the countryside.

Constantine

# LIFE IN THE COUNTRY

ALTHOUGH the Romans developed towns in Britain for the first time, most of the population still went on living in the country. It is difficult to work out what the total population of Roman Britain was (estimates vary between half a million and one and a half million), but it seems clear that the 33 civil towns – that is, proper towns as distinct from military settlements such as are found along Hadrian's Wall – had a population of less than 200,000. The rest of the population consisted almost entirely of farmers, farm-workers, and their families.

The Roman country house is usually known as a villa, which is simply the Latin word for 'farm'; but it is not a word we can use of every house in the country where Romano-British people happened to live. In some of the more remote areas which were ruled by the Roman military government, local farmers went on living in a way that was hardly changed at all by the new civilization. For example, at Chysauster in Cornwall, in the far-off west of Britain, a group of stone hut circles still survives; in these six rough houses, built of dry-stone masonry, a group of Celtic farmers lived. Some of them probably mined for the local tin as well, and sold it to merchants. But these huts, and similar ones in the north of England, in Wales and in Scotland, could never be called 'villas', though they were inhabited right through Roman times.

Among all the many Roman country houses that are known in Britain – and over 700 of them have been identified so far, with many more probably still to be discovered – the biggest contrast with the huts at Chysauster is to be found at one of the earliest villas built. This villa is so big and grand, in fact, that it has been called a palace. It is at Fishbourne, a mile and half west of Chichester in Sussex. Very soon after Claudius's invasion in A.D. 43, Claudius had made the king of these parts, a man called Cogidubnus, a Roman citizen: Cogidubnus even took the name Claudius as his own second name. He was probably related to Verica, the chieftain who had fled to Rome, and it was useful for the Romans to have a friendly ally in the early years of the occupation, especially along the Sussex coast.

It seems that very early on a harbour was organized at Fishbourne, so that military supplies could be brought in by the Romans to the camp they had built at Chichester. Timber buildings were made as storage places. But once the army had conquered lowland England, and the Romans felt safe there, these buildings were abandoned and gradually a new and splendid kind of building was constructed, large, made of stone, and using some of the most luxurious features of which the Romans were capable.

Archaeologists think it likely that this palace at Fishbourne, which was put up in the decade A.D. 60–70, was specially made for Cogidubnus as a reward for his help. Certainly the size, craftsmanship and lavish magnificence of the building all seem to point to it being a royal dwelling (see colour plate 7). Its architectural layout is more like the great country houses of Italy than other villas in Britain. First there was an impressive waiting hall, its roof mounted on six enormous columns at the front. Beyond it was a pool, a large garden, and at the far end of the garden the west wing of the palace, raised up so as to overlook the rest, and flanked on each side by the north and south wings, long colonnades behind which were the living quarters. Inside, no expense was spared on the decoration of the rooms. Marble was brought from as far away as Turkey, Greece, Italy and Spain, and was used for the door and window frames and laid into some of the walls. Other walls had moulded stucco friezes, decorated with birds. There were more than 60 mosaics on the floors: some had geometrical patterns laid out in black and white – regular crosses, triangles, rectangles and squares – and others were in many colours, arranged in bands of rosettes and vine leaves. There were wall paintings on the stucco, one of them showing a colonnaded villa against the background of the sea.

When the archaeologists were digging at Fishbourne palace during the 1960s, their most remarkable discovery was the remains of the vast garden, very carefully and regularly laid out. The plan of this was known because the Roman gardeners dug deep trenches into which they bedded the shrubs in compost, and the trenches survive (see plate 17). So the whole arrangement of shrubs, trees and hedges could be worked out, as well as the paths that went round the garden, the pipes through which water was led, and the decorative marble basins into which the water ran and which were placed along the paths. Because all this is known, the gardens have now been restored to look just as they would have done when the house was inhabited.

Cogidubnus probably died towards the end of the first century A.D., and – if he was indeed the proud owner of the Fishbourne palace – we have no idea who succeeded him there. But we do know that the palace went on being added to and altered during the next two centuries. Although the original palace had a suite of baths in the south-eastern part, a new suite of baths was built in the north wing, with its walls painted red and white. New mosaic floors were laid, including one showing the head of Medusa, black, red and yellow, with snakes writhing out of her hair. Another was designed with sea-horses, a cupid riding on a dolphin, and some very odd-looking winged panthers swimming in the sea (see colour plate 8). One of the later additions was a hypocaust system: strangely enough, the original palace was not centrally heated, perhaps because the architects were from Italy and weren't used to the special needs of the cold British climate. And it may have been the hypocaust furnace that caused a disastrous fire towards the end of the third century A.D.

Whatever the cause, the fire did terrible damage. The timbers in the roofs collapsed, bringing down a great weight of roof tiles; the lead used for roof fittings melted and fell in puddles on the floors; the glass window panes shattered in the heat. Charcoal and ash covered everything. Archaeologists could tell that people

17. Excavated bedding trenches at Fishbourne

came back after the fire and looked in the ruins for anything that had managed to survive it, because the roof beams and tiles had been disturbed by being lifted. But the palace was not rebuilt. It was pulled down, any building stone that could be used again was taken away, and the grass began to grow over the rubble. Where the palace had been became fields. It was not until 1960 that a workman, digging a trench for a water-main, came across a lot of Roman tiles under the earth, told the archaeologists, and so started the rediscovery of this amazing building and its garden.

Though the palace at Fishbourne is exceptional, there are many other large Romano-British villas which were the houses of rich farmers. Not far from Fishbourne, at Bignor, north of Chichester, are the remains of one of them. What is typical about it is the way in which it shows how a successful family (and one can imagine how a farm would be handed on from generation to generation) gradually made elaborate improvements to the original simple plan. First of all at Bignor there was a wooden cottage with only five rooms. Then a front corridor was added, and a couple of rooms as wings off it. This 'corridor house' (as they are called) was then converted into a much larger set of buildings round a courtyard, rather like a less grand version of the Fishbourne palace. And then, in the fourth century A.D., more splendid rooms were built, with very fine mosaic floors showing cupids pretending to be gladiators, the boy Ganymede being carried off by an eagle, dancing women, and the goddess Venus.

Most Roman villas, and nearly all the most important ones, are found in the lowlands of southern England, where the best farming land was and where life was most settled: round London, on the south coast, in Hampshire, the Isle of Wight and the Cotswolds. The settlers were careful in choosing the right spot for their villas: often on a sheltered slope, out of the wind and catching as much sun as possible, close to a good water supply, and with a pleasant view of the countryside round about. The largest of them were set in the middle of big estates: the villa at Ditchley in Oxfordshire belonged to a family that farmed at least a thousand acres. In the most favoured areas, a large number of villas are found quite close together: within a ten-mile radius of Chedworth villa (in Gloucestershire, and one of the best villas in Britain), about 22 others have been found. Most of them lie fairly close to a Roman highway, though the tracks or lanes to each of them were not proper roads and must have been made by local labour.

The villas and the towns depended on each other, with the farm produce from the villa estates being taken to the nearest town and sold in the market. Wheat was the chief crop, with much smaller amounts of rye and barley, and of course large quantities of vegetables and fruit – though one of our commonest vegetables nowadays, the potato, was not brought into Britain until Elizabethan times. Clover and grass were cut for cattle feed, and cows, sheep, goats, pigs and horses were raised. Milk, cheese and honey (the only form of sweetening) were manufactured on the farms. Wool was one of the most important products, particularly in the Cotswolds.

The equipment used on the villa estates was simple by our standards, but it was an improvement on the tools which the British had had on their small farms before the coming of the Romans. The iron ploughshares and coulters of the Romans were bigger and better grooved to fit the shaft (see plate 18); and there was even a kind of mechanical harvester (a vallus) – an ox-drawn wagon into which a board set with wooden teeth was fixed, which tore off the ears of corn and dropped them into a box. Scythes, sickles, spades, rakes, hoes, picks and ploughshares have all been found on the sites of Roman villas in Britain.

One of the biggest jobs the Romans did was the draining of the Fens in eastern England. This was probably organized by Roman army engineers, and may have been partly carried out by soldiers. Deep channels, canals and ditches were built to drain away the water, and on the land that was recovered small farms were built – though no fine villas have been found in these areas, and it is thought that the farmers may have only been tenants who worked on land that was rented from the government. The drainage system needed constant care and renewal, and one of the many effects of the collapse of Roman civilization in Britain (which you

18. Bronze Roman model of plough drawn by oxen found in
County Durham

will read about in the last chapter of this book) was that the Fens
filled up with water again and became a wilderness for more than
a thousand years.

The villa itself was of course the home of the landowner. We
know very little about the life of the ordinary farm workers, who
would have lived in much simpler houses, not much different
from those of their ancestors before the Roman invasion. So we
must remember that the picture we have nowadays of Romano-
British country life is concentrated on the habits and tastes of the
comparatively rich. As Tacitus remarked, in a piece I quoted
from earlier, the appeal of Roman civilization was a very real
one to the British who accepted Roman rule, particularly to the
chieftains or aristocratic class who stood to gain most from it.
Just as the public baths were an attractive novelty in the towns,

and soon became regarded as a necessity, so in the villas a great deal of money and effort was put into the building of private bath-houses. Sometimes these were extremely grand – so much so, indeed, that at Chedworth the elaborate system of hot water tanks, cold plunge-baths and equipment of the sort you find in modern sauna baths, was originally considered by archaeologists to be a large workshop for the preparation and dyeing of coloured woollen cloth. Yet the fact is that the owners of Chedworth thought it worthwhile to have such a modern and expensive set of baths for their own private use.

In the same way, they must have spent a great deal on mosaics. Although the early mosaic craftsman came to Britain from other parts of the Roman Empire, by the fourth century A.D. there were four chief workshops in Britain itself, each with its own style: by the river Humber in Yorkshire, at Water Newton in Northamptonshire, at Cirencester, and at Dorchester in Dorset. The most splendid mosaic in Britain is at Woodchester in Gloucestershire. It was made by the Cirencester workshop, is 50 feet square, shows Orpheus, Neptune, water nymphs and all kind of animals, and is so precious that it is uncovered and put on show only every ten years, so that it can be protected from frost and other weather damage.

Other kinds of rich decoration found in villas are wall mosaics, painted wall plaster, particularly good at Lullingstone villa in Kent (see colour plate 13), and marble sculptures, such as the two busts, perhaps of father and son, which were also found at Lullingstone and which would have stood in niches in the wall of the main room – family portraits, in fact (see plate 19). One sign of how superior owners like these must have felt to their ancestors is the way in which villas not only gradually extend, with new wings and suites, but also begin to have quite separate living quarters cut off from the servants and farm offices, with their own courtyards and ornamental gardens, so that it seems some of these owners can be called 'gentlemen farmers'; they would have farm managers and overseers, while they themselves would enjoy the country pleasures of hunting and perhaps quite frequent visits to town.

19. One of the two marble busts found at Lullingstone villa, Kent

Although we have no descriptions by their owners of villas in Britain, many Roman writers elsewhere in the Empire left accounts of the pleasures of country life. Seneca (the writer who told about all the noises that disturbed him in the bath-house) described a particular farm in Italy like this:

> It is built of squared stone; there are trees round it, and a wall round them; at either end rises a tower, flanking the house; below the buildings and their clump of greenery lies a reservoir large enough to water an army.

And Horace the poet, who had a farm outside Rome which he used to go to when he wanted to get away from the noise and hurry of the city, wrote a verse letter to a friend about it:

> My dear friend Quinctius, you ask about my farm –
> if it enriches its master with ploughland or with olives,
> with fruit or pastures or with elm trees clothed in vines:
> so let me lovingly sketch its shape and situation.
> Unbroken hills, just once divided by a dark
> valley: the sun approaching looks on the right side,
> departing, warms the left with the rays of his vanishing chariot.
> You'd praise the temperate air. And think of this! – the kindly
> bushes bear wild plums and cherries, the oak and ilex
> delight the cattle with their acorns, me with their shade . . .
> There is a spring besides, worthy to name a river:
> Hebrus, wandering through Thrace, is no purer or colder.
> Its flow will cure distempered heads and sickly stomachs.
> That is my hidden home: dear, yes, and beautiful.

Of course the olives and the grapevines would not have been an obvious feature of a villa in Britain (indeed the olive was not grown here, and though in some sheltered parts of the southeast there were vines, most of the wine which was so much part of Roman life was imported from warmer parts of the Empire); and shade from the sun was more important in the Mediterranean countries than it was in the most northerly province. But there must have been several wealthy but country-loving villa owners in Britain who felt as Horace did. We can even imagine some of them commuting to the nearest town, to work as officials – perhaps as magistrates in the basilica – and then hurrying thankfully back to their rural retreats.

·　·　·　·　·

This kind of life was very different not only from that of the farm workers and from that of the old-type farm settlements on the western and northern edges of the settled areas, but also from another kind of country life – that of the soldiers who guarded and patrolled the frontiers. For many years these frontiers went on changing, as the armies pushed north and west and conquered the troublesome tribes. In these parts the soldiers sometimes built temporary camps, which they used when they were training or on manoeuvres, but even in these cases they constructed the defences so solidly that air photographs can reveal them, such as the group of 'practice camps' at Cawthorn in North Yorkshire (see plate 20).

After the first conquest of the Brigantes in Yorkshire and the conquest of the tribes in Wales, the main enemy lay far to the north. In A.D. 122, the Emperor Hadrian (see plates 21 and 25) visited Britain, and that year began the construction of the enormous wall named after him. It runs from the Tyne in the east to the Solway in the west, and was built between the time of Hadrian's visit and the year 133. For 73 miles this huge defensive frontier ran across country, with towers and barracks at regular intervals. Seventeen forts were built on or close to the wall (see colour plates 9a and 9b) on each of which was based a cavalry regiment or infantry battalion. It was a frontier which was intended for attack as well as defence, and from it the Roman troops went on campaigns even further north.

Such a vast army, though linked by road to such important northern cities as York, needed to be able to look after itself for much of the time. So there grew up, close to the wall, a number of fortress-settlements (see plate 22) which were like neither the civilian towns nor the villas. There were bath-houses and shops, temples and bars, breweries and places of entertainment – but all of these were intended solely for the army and the many people who worked behind the lines to provide food and drink for the troops, to repair their equipment, and to do all the other necessary jobs that a permanent military force needs. It seems that at least some of the officers had their wives and children with them, and these would live in the fortress-settlements – such as Vindolanda,

which lies a mile south of the wall and about 20 miles east of
Carlisle.

20. Aerial view of Roman camps at Cawthorn

21. Bronze head of Hadrian

The excavations of the settlement at Vindolanda have given us a good idea of what life in these remote northern settlements must

22. Roman fort and civil settlement outside it at Old Carlisle, Cumbria

have been like. One of the most surprising things is that living conditions seem to have been much dirtier and less well organized than you might have expected from the Romans. In the house of the military commander at Vindolanda, bracken had been piled up on the floor as a covering: when it got filthy, it was not replaced but more bracken was thrown down on top of the old, and flies in their thousands bred in this rubbish. Yet there are bath-houses here, as you would suppose, and the commander must have been a civilized man. Perhaps he felt so far from civilization that he grew careless and let his personal standards of cleanliness and order slip.

The most remarkable objects found so far at Vindolanda have been a large number of wooden writing tablets (see plate 23). Until excavations began on the site in the early 1970s, only one such tablet had been found in Britain, far away in Somerset: at Vindolanda over a hundred have turned up, preserved in the

23. Wooden writing tablet from Vindolanda

strange conditions of the damp peaty soil, along with leather sandals and fragments of clothing – just the sort of material that usually disappears. The very thin, very small Vindolanda tablets were sometimes covered with wax (on which words would be scratched), sometimes they were written onto direct with pen and ink. The actual writing is of course now very faint, and the handwriting itself is in a difficult style, but gradually they are being deciphered. So far there seems to be a mixture of private letters and lists of military stores – requisitions for food, equipment and so on. The sort of thing we can expect to find on some of the tablets is information and gossip such as that recorded on a fragment of a letter found in London, ending with the words: 'And mind you turn that slave-girl into cash'.

About ten years after the completion of Hadrian's Wall, the Emperor Antoninus Pius (see plate 24) decided to push the frontier even further north. Another great wall was built, this time between the Firth of Forth and the Firth of Clyde in Scotland. This is the so-called Antonine Wall. But it was much more exposed to the northern tribes, and by the end of the second century A.D. it was abandoned. Hadrian's Wall survived, however, and was manned by troops up until not long before the final withdrawal of the Roman armies from Britain.

24. Antoninus Pius

It is known that Legions from several different parts of the Empire were stationed in garrisons on both walls, and it must have been a particularly grim experience for soldiers who came from such hot countries as Spain. The mists and fogs, the seemingly endless rain, the miserable cold – all these must have been even worse than the rebellious tribes to the north which they were meant to keep under control. The twentieth-century poet, W. H. Auden, imagined in his poem 'Roman Wall Blues' what such a soldier might glumly sing to himself as he patrolled the frontier:

> Over the heather the wet wind blows,
> I've lice in my tunic and a cold in my nose.
>
> The rain comes pattering out of the sky,
> I'm a Wall soldier, I don't know why.
>
> The mist creeps over the hard grey stone,
> My girl's in Tungria; I sleep alone. . . .
>
> She gave me a ring but I diced it away;
> I want my girl and I want my pay.
>
> When I'm a veteran with only one eye
> I shall do nothing but look at the sky.

From Syria and Spain, from Gaul and Germany, soldiers came to garrison these heavily fortified and entrenched areas. Behind them lay the towns, the villas, the cultivated fields, and over 7,000 miles of roads in Britain alone. But up on the northern frontier, on the Wall, all these must have seemed a very long way off.

My mention of the Roman roads leads me on to say something about these long-lasting monuments, which are probably the most common everyday reminders of the Roman settlement in Britain, even when we don't immediately recognise them. The countryside is covered with a thick network of them. If you look at a map of Roman Britain (see map on page 16), you see them fan out from the main towns, linking town with town, going as far north as the forward military outposts beyond the Antonine Wall, and in the south-west almost as far as Lands End in Cornwall. The villas are little dots that lie back from them. If you put a map of the modern road system next to the Roman one, you see that many present-day roads follow the same routes as the old: the Roman military engineers judged well the lie of the land. They also built so solidly that even when the routes themselves have been abandoned, clear traces of them can often be seen today, running across fields, going side by side with hedges, walls and other more recent boundaries, the raised embankments (aggers) on which they were laid standing up above the surrounding fields. The surfaces of most of these are completely overgrown now, but there are a few which still show well-preserved paving stones. The best stretch is on Blackstone Edge in the Pennines, where in hilly country an exposed section of road 16 feet wide runs down a steep slope. There are kerbs, and down the middle of the road is a deep worn groove, which it is thought may have been caused by the constant rubbing of brake-poles on carts going down the hill (see plate 26).

Milestones were placed along the main highways, and bridges built over rivers – though often the engineers made use whenever they could of natural fords. One of the most important roads,

26. Section of Roman road at Blackstone Edge

which we call the Fosse Way (see plate 27), was originally as much an indication of the frontier as a road: running across Britain diagonally from Exeter to Lincoln, it marked off the peaceful lowlands from the military zone. Roman roads are known for their straightness, and when they changed direction they usually did so abruptly, without wandering about as so many medieval country roads do.

The Romans themselves had road maps, such as the Antonine Itinerary, which dates from the late second or early third century A.D. and which gives lists of places on the various routes and the distances between them. Another slightly later one is the Tabula Peutingeriana, which marks all the roads as red lines. When there is no obvious sign of a Roman road today, certain place names on modern maps can give clues that there are likely to be traces of a road somewhere. When the Saxons came – and the Saxons were certainly not road builders – they used their word *streat* of these impressively paved surfaces; and from this we get such place names as Streatham, Stratford, Stratton, Stretton, and indeed Street itself. The name *stan* or *stone* often hints at the same thing – Stanstead, Stanford, and so on. And because the roads were embanked and stood up above the country, we find such names as Ridgeway and Causeway (including Devil's Causeway, which seems to show that later inhabitants thought the Devil himself must have been responsible for building such formidable highways).

With all this talk of roads and highways, you must not suppose that the majority of ordinary people in Roman Britain did much travelling. The highways were built in the first place for military and government communications, and, though merchants would use them as well, the country people probably had little cause – and not much opportunity – to go from place to place. The estates of the villas were worked by slaves, and also serfs – that is, farm workers who were given some right to shelter, food and protection in return for what they did for their master. Slavery existed in Britain before the Romans, but the buying and selling

27. The Fosse Way, near Easton Grey, Wiltshire

of slaves was more rigidly controlled under the Roman Empire; it was also quite common for a master to free a number of his slaves, or for them to buy their freedom. Slaves and serfs were not necessarily badly treated; whether they were or not depended on how kind or otherwise the villa owner was. But whatever he was like, most country workers would know only their fields and the area close by, and perhaps the local town.

Skilled workers who had learned a craft – weaving, spinning, masonry, making farm tools and repairing them – would of course have a better and more privileged life than those who could only dig, hoe, gather the crops at harvest time, or look after the farm animals as shepherds and goatherds and cattle hands. The women were cooks, house servants, washers and cleaners, and sometimes helped with the children of the villa owner. In all these activities, and in the way in which they were regarded, their life cannot have been very different from that which their ancestors led in the households of tribal chieftains before the Roman invasion, or indeed from the kind of life their descendants went on leading in Britain for centuries to come. The difference lies mainly in the organization and standardization of Romano-British life, which meant in effect that life on the estates of a villa in Gloucestershire was very like that on the estates of villas in Gaul, in Spain, in Yugoslavia and North Africa. The climate varied, the crops varied, to some extent clothing varied; but rural life on such estates was far more similar than otherwise. The villa buildings, the mosaics inside, the best dinner service of Samian ware, the jewellery worn by the master's wife, the methods for heating the hypocaust and pumping water and ploughing the land – all these were the same, with small variations, throughout the whole vast Roman Empire. It was a kind of uniformity that had not existed before, and would not really exist again until the Industrial Revolution.

25. Hadrian

꩜꩜꩜꩜꩜꩜

# PLEASURES AND PURSUITS

꩜꩜꩜꩜꩜꩜

FOR most people in Roman Britain, as for most people at most times, work had to be the main activity in life, whether in town or country. Soldiers, farmers, craftsmen, government officials, shopkeepers, servants, labourers and slaves – all were part of a highly organized society which needed hard work and efficient administration if it was to run smoothly. But there had to be times of relaxation too. It was a Roman playwright, Terence, who wrote: 'The human mind always runs downhill from toil to pleasure', and a Roman poet, Juvenal, who said that there are only two things people really want – *Panem et circenses* ('bread and circuses'). Having earned their food, they wanted to eat it at leisure and to enjoy themselves.

Of course we know much more about the eating habits of rich Romans than we do about the ordinary people, partly because there are written accounts in Latin of splendid meals in fine houses. The best villas in Britain had a separate dining-room, the triclinium, in which couches were laid out round a low table from which the food would be served. But this would happen only for dinner at the end of the day, which might begin to be eaten at any time between four in the afternoon and seven in the evening. The midday meal was not important, and often breakfast was simply a drink of water and perhaps some fruit.

In the kitchens, servants used charcoal to heat the stoves and the fireplace, and prepared the food with implements many of which are versions of things we still use; though of course much more preparation was needed than in our time of canned and frozen foods. One of the commonest kinds of pottery found at any place where the Romans lived is pieces of mortaria: these were large, strong bowls which were used for pounding and grinding food, and the inner surface is usually roughened with grit mixed with the clay to help this. One side is opened out so that whatever it held could be poured from it. These mortaria often carry the name of the manufacturer, stamped on the rim while the clay was still soft. Other things found are kitchen knives, cleavers for cutting up joints of meat, iron hooks and chains for holding cooking pots above a fire, strainers for vegetables, presses used for making cheese, big wine jars (amphorae), and every kind of bowl, jug, basin, cup and plate (see plate 28 and colour plate 10). At table, there were spoons and knives, but the fork, oddly enough, was little used.

An elaborate banquet might go on for hours. The gustatio – the first course, designed to whet your appetite – could consist of a lightly spiced egg dish, or a small salad, or some shellfish: oysters were very popular, not only with the rich, and on most

28. Roman table and kitchen utensils

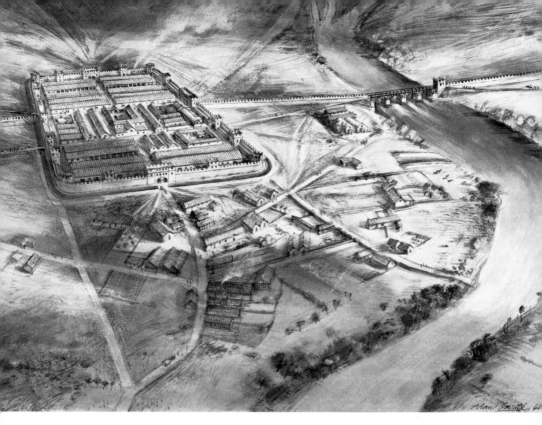

9a. Reconstruction of Chesters Roman fort, Hadrian's Wall

9b. Aerial view of Chesters Roman fort today

10. Roman pottery from Wroxeter

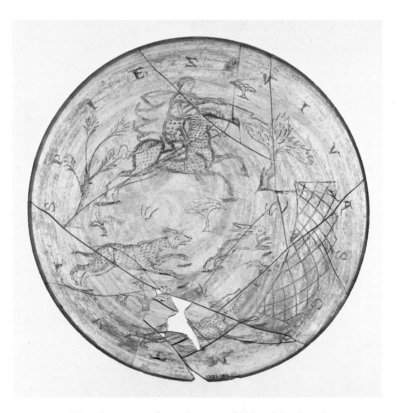

11. Hunting scene from imported Rhenish glass bowl,
found in Somerset

Roman sites in Britain oyster shells are found in large quantities. Colchester was the chief port for them, and most towns had stalls selling them, where they could either be taken away or eaten on the spot. Another favourite food to start the meal was snails, which were commonly fattened on milk. The large edible snail (the kind the French, for example, still eat) was first brought into Britain by the Romans.

The main course would be meat and vegetables. Pork was a favourite meat, and also wild boar. Boar hunts were popular among the Roman officers: in Britain an altar has been found on wild moorland, with an inscription saying that it was set up by a cavalry commander to the god Silvanus, and that the commander 'was grateful for taking a wild boar of remarkable fineness which many of his predecessors had been unable to bag'. Birds of many kinds were eaten (including exotic ones, such as the peacock and – though not in Britain – the ostrich), but less beef and lamb than nowadays. At the end of the meal, sweet pastries were served, and fruit.

Different kinds of wine were drunk throughout the meal. In Britain most of the wine was imported from Italy and Gaul, since there were not the right conditions in the island's cold climate for growing grapes successfully: beer was the local drink. But a rich villa household undoubtedly bought imported wines, and amphorae in which the wine was contained have been found all over Britain. The wine was poured from these into jugs or large bowls (sometimes through strainers to catch the sediment), and from there into small cups or shallow drinking bowls, often made of the shiny red Samian pottery. Some beakers have been found in Britain which have cheerful drinking remarks painted on them – BIBE (Drink!), SUAVIS (Sweet, or Smooth), DA MI (Give it to me!), MISCE MIHI (Mix for me!), NOLITE SITIRE (Don't be thirsty!), and VIVATIS (Long life!). The remark about mixing refers to the fact that wine was often mixed with a little water before being served.

Hunting of all kinds was enjoyed, for both food and sport. Many designs on Roman pots show hunting scenes, with everything from deer to hares being pursued, often with a pack of hunting dogs, which are also shown (see colour plate 11). A particular kind of Romano-British pottery, which archaeologists call Castor Ware or Nene Valley Ware (after the place in Northamptonshire where it was manufactured), is full of such hunting scenes. The favourite dog in these is a type of greyhound, obviously valued for its speed. For those who preferred the gentler pleasures of fishing, both the sea and rivers were used. Mosaics and carvings show fishermen in boats and on river banks, and both fish hooks and needles for making and mending nets have been found.

Whenever the pleasures of the Romans are thought of, most people immediately remember something about the cruel slaughter of men and of animals in the amphitheatres – the 'circuses' of Juvenal's remark. To begin with, before the establishment of Roman civilization, such death games were part of the funeral rituals of the Etruscans in Italy; and it is thought that the spilling of blood in this way was intended to be a sacrifice to please the gods. By the time Roman Britain was settled, however, any religious significance had been long forgotten, though of course the gladiatorial fights and wild-beast hunts that took place in the amphitheatres had their own rituals. The gladiators were usually slaves, war prisoners or criminals, who were sometimes given the chance to win their freedom by behaving with particular bravery and skill in front of the crowd. One kind of gladiator, the mirmillo, wore a heavy crested helmet of Greek type and carried a short sword. Another kind, the retiarius, used a net (in which to entangle his opponent) and a three-pronged spear or trident, like Neptune, the sea god. In Britain, pictures of gladiators have been found decorating all kinds of objects – pottery (see plate 29), glass beakers, mosaics, and also small bronze figurines of them, which were perhaps souvenirs from the amphitheatre.

It seems certain that gladiatorial fights went on in Britain, in the amphitheatres which have been found – at Caerleon (see plate 30) and Chester (where the audience was probably military), near Dorchester in Dorset, at Cirencester, Silchester, Chichester,

29. Gladiators on vase, from Colchester

Richborough (Kent) and Caerwent. Fights between wild beasts were perhaps not so common as they were in, say, North Africa (which controlled the trade in strange and fierce beasts from the south) and in Rome itself: it would have been expensive to transport lions and tigers all the way to the remote northern province. But bulls and bears were no doubt baited (both of them were native to Britain, the bear not yet having been exterminated), just as they were right down until the middle of the seventeenth century.

30. Roman military amphitheatre at Caerleon

Nowadays we are of course shocked by the useless bloodshed and cruelty of these gladiatorial displays and torture of animals – though bullfighting manages to survive and flourish even now in Spain. What we ought to remember is that there must always have been a minority of people in Roman times also who disliked them. In his *Confessions*, written towards the end of the fourth century A.D., Augustine of Hippo (in North Africa) spoke of this 'cruel and bloodthirsty sport', and gave a very good picture of a friend of his, Alypius, who was reluctantly taken by some fellow students to the arena:

> When they arrived at the arena, the place was seething with a lust for cruelty. They found seats as best they could and Alypius shut his eyes tightly, determined to have nothing to do with these atrocities. If only he had closed his ears as well! For an incident in the fight drew a great roar from the crowd, and this thrilled him so deeply that he could not contain his curiosity . . . When he saw the blood, it was as though he had drunk a deep draught of savage passion. Instead of turning away, he fixed his eyes upon the scene and drank in all its frenzy, unaware what he was doing. He revelled in the wickedness of the fighting and was drunk with the fascination of bloodshed. He was no longer the man who had come to the arena, but simply one of the crowd which he had joined, a fit companion for the friends who had brought him.

This vivid passage gives a clear impression of the way in which the excitement of the crowd could spread even to someone who knew that what went on in these arenas and amphitheatres was disgusting.

The true 'circus', in the Latin sense, was the place where chariot races were held. These were tremendously popular in Rome (where the charioteers had their own supporters' clubs – the Reds, the Whites, the Blues and the Greens), but so far no remains of a circus have been found in Roman Britain. However, British horses were famous, so it is likely that circuses existed; and there are a number of representations of chariots and chariot races on mosaics, cups and sculptures. A piece of sculpture found at Lincoln shows a boy driving a chariot (see plate 31), and a mosaic

31. Fragment of sculpture showing a boy driving a chariot, from Lincoln

from Horkstow in Lincolnshire has four panels showing different stages in a chariot race. In one of them, a horse has broken away from its chariot, and a man on horseback is galloping after it with a lasso to try to recapture it.

There were plenty of quieter ways of enjoyment too. Music, for example. Though little is known about Roman composition and instruments, a bronze figure of a woman playing a kind of pipe called a tibia (found at Silchester) shows they enjoyed making music (see plate 32). The Romans were fond of all kinds of games; even more than various games of handball and football, they

loved games with dice and board games. Counters made of
pottery, bone and glass have been found in many parts of Roman
Britain: these were used on boards divided up into squares, in
games that were like versions of chess or draughts, and such
boards have been found in north Wales, in Kent, at Chester, and
along Hadrian's Wall. One dice that turned up was weighted in
such a way that the six almost always fell when it was thrown,
which suggests that the gambler who owned it was quite prepared
to cheat.

32. Bronze figure of a woman playing the tibia, found at Silchester

Children had toys, of course, and though a number of these were probably dolls made of wood and cloth which has rotted away, dolls and miniature animals made of pottery and bronze have been found. At York, a little girl's grave contained a tiny bronze mouse which had been buried with her (see plate 33). Several bronze dogs have been found (see plates 34a and b), and we know from a variety of sources that pet animals were commonly kept and much loved: dogs, cats, hares, birds. Quite often during excavations on Roman sites floor tiles are found which had been walked over by animals while the tiles were still damp before being fired and hardened in the kiln. One of the most amusing is in the museum at Verulamium: evidently a dog was standing on one of these damp tiles when someone saw him, and three marks can be seen there – the paw marks of the dog when he was standing still, then a pebble buried in the clay, and then the blurred marks made by the dog as he ran quickly off, frightened by whoever threw the stone at him.

33. Bronze mouse found in a child's grave at York

Reading was not such a common pleasure, for two main reasons. One was that there were no printed books, and all books and pieces of writing had to be copied by hand – a slow and expensive business, so that only the rich could afford books. And along with this went the fact that many people in Roman Britain were probably illiterate. Officials, merchants, villa owners doing their farm accounts, most (but not all) army officers – these

34a and b. Bronze dogs, probably children's toys, found at Carrawburgh
and Kirkby Thore

would need to be able to read and write. But for most people it was not necessary. Education was very advanced in the central Roman Empire – Italy, Gaul, and so on – but it had to be paid for, so that those who could not afford school fees for their children had to do without. We can only guess that Roman Britain too had schools, but there is no trace of them.

What we do know is that some quite ordinary people had managed to pick up enough education to be able to write at least a few words (see colour plate 6) – words which survive scratched on walls, tiles, and bits of broken pottery. These graffiti (the name for words scratched, rather than carved, on the surface of anything) are among the most human bits of the past we have: reading them seems to put you more directly in touch with these distant people than anything else that survives. The most famous of them, famous because we can only guess what sort of incident lay behind the words, was found scratched on a tile in London: it says AUSTALIS DIBUS XIII VAGATUR SIBI COTIDIM which means 'Austalis has been going off on his own every day for thirteen days'. Perhaps Austalis was miserably in love with someone, or perhaps he was lazy, or perhaps he was just feeling moody. We shall never know.

A tile from Silchester has a bit of Virgil's poetry scratched on it, so it may have been part of a writing lesson; or perhaps a student trying to do some revision before an exam. A brickmaker in Silchester wrote on a box tile (used in the walls in houses where there was a hypocaust system) 'Clementinus made this box tile'. Another wrote 'Primus has made ten tiles'. At Caerwent, a tile was found which seems to have been used for a writing lesson, because someone wrote on it the name *Bellicianus*, and underneath it there are three copies of the same name, each in a different style. The oddest piece of writing is also from Caerwent: a section of wall plaster, on which can be seen (but not read) the traces of something someone had written – but someone else had evidently been shocked or annoyed by the words, because the scribble has been rubbed away, and underneath it is the word *puniamini* – 'May you be punished!'

These pleasures, and the added skill of writing (for the pre-Roman Celts had no form of writing), were the sort of thing Tacitus meant in that mocking passage I quoted in Chapter Two – about 'the luxuries that make vice pleasant – arcades, baths, and splendid banquets'. Tacitus says that the British became fond of these, of Roman clothes, of the Latin language. He wrote too early to know how deeply all these Roman 'novelties' would be absorbed by Romano-Britains – or to predict how completely they would be swept away in the end, as the whole Roman Empire began to disintegrate in the centuries long after his death.

Pendant made of jet, found at York

# CUSTOM AND CEREMONY

᠗᠗᠗᠗᠗᠗

THE ways in which the dead are buried tell us something about the beliefs of the living. This is true of people all over the world, and at all times. So archaeologists have always attached great importance to the excavation of burials, because the treatment of the body, the things which may be put in the grave with it, and any memorial which was put there, are all pieces of evidence about the religious ideas of the time and place.

The Romans, as I have said already, were usually tolerant of whatever religions they came across in the lands they conquered and occupied; so long as the peace was kept and Roman order acknowledged, they were willing not only to accept the local gods but often to adapt them to their own. The religious beliefs and practices followed in the Roman Empire were very varied, from the most primitive pagan worship of trees and stones to Christianity, which spread from its beginnings in the small and rather insignificant Roman province of Judea to affect most of the world. In Roman Britain we can find signs of both, and many others besides.

Most of our knowledge of Romano-British religions has been learned from burials, though I shall come to what we have discovered from temples, sculpture, mosaics, etc. a little later. Almost always the burials are found outside the towns or other settlements. One of the most ancient Roman laws, which applied throughout the Roman Empire, was: 'Thou shalt not bury or burn a dead man within a city'. The reasons for this were practical rather than religious, to do with health dangers and the cost of land, not belief. At the time of Claudius's conquest in A.D. 43, and for at least another century, the Romans cremated their dead. The ashes and burnt bone were then put in a container (usually a pottery jar or a square glass bottle) and buried in a grave in a cemetery. Sometimes – with the poorer people – the grave was just a hole in the ground, without any protection or any kind of monument above it. But in many cases the hole was lined with slabs of stone, or tiles, and a tombstone was placed above it.

These cremation burials sometimes have a coin or a few pottery dishes buried with the ashes, but the sort of elaborate 'grave goods' that are found in so many other ancient burials (not only the Egyptians but also the Bronze Age and Iron Age inhabitants of Britain) were never part of Roman customs. The Romans varied a good deal, both individually and from age to age, in their ideas about whether there was some kind of life after death. By the third century A.D., there was a fairly general belief that in some way the body survived, so that some useful things in the grave might be necessary, if only to take on the journey to the next world. From this time on we find burials of the complete body, together with some grave goods – dishes for food and drink, a few ornaments that the dead person had worn, in the case of children some toys, and often a coin placed in the mouth of the skull. This coin was to pay the fare to Charon, who was supposed to ferry people in his boat across the river Styx to the land of the dead. But weapons, for example, are very seldom found in Romano-British graves, even in the graves of soldiers; and when they are, the graves usually belong to troops who came from parts of the Empire in which some people still clung to old beliefs, long since forgotten elsewhere.

It seems that the most important thing the Romans wanted to show in a burial was that those who were left loved and honoured the dead person – and they wanted to show this to the living world as much as to the next one. The simplest form of inscription on a tombstone begins with the words *Dis Manibus* or DM – 'to the spirits of the departed' (see plate 35) – and goes on to give the name and the age of the person. Very often some

35. Tombstone of Julia Velva, York

words follow saying who had put up the stone – the widow, widower, son, daughter; or sometimes a master to his slave, or a slave to his master. A common ending to the inscription is H.S.E. (short for *Hic situs est* – 'He is laid here'). Tombstones of soldiers usually give details of where they came from, which military unit they had served with, and how long they had served. One from Wroxeter (the Roman Viroconium) reads: 'Marcus Petronius, son of Lucius, of the Menenian tribe, from Vicetia, aged 38, soldier of the Fourteenth Legion Gemina, served 18 years, was a standard-bearer and is buried here'.

Whether they believed in some kind of bodily resurrection or not, almost all Romans thought that the spirit of the dead survived, even if only in some vague and shadowy way. If the proper ceremonies were not performed when someone died, the spirit might come back, troubled or angry, and haunt the relatives who for whatever reason had not followed the correct rituals. Some people believed in the old Greek idea that the spirits of the dead returned to earth in other forms, inhabiting another body. In the case of very famous and splendid people, the spirit might even become a star: the poet Ovid wrote about the soul of Julius Caesar turning into a comet when he was assassinated. Another poet, Virgil, wrote in detail in his long poem, the *Aeneid*, about the journey through the underworld of his hero Aeneas, who recognized there people he knew on earth.

As far as the government of the Roman Empire was concerned, the spirit of the Emperor himself was the most important part of religion. Since the time of Augustus (who succeeded Julius Caesar), the Emperor had been officially regarded as a god: his *numen*, or spiritual power, was worshipped. We have seen already how the great temple at Colchester was built and dedicated to Claudius very soon after the Roman conquest. After it was destroyed during Boudicca's revolt, it was rebuilt and went on being used as a centre for what is known as the 'Imperial Cult'. There were other temples at York and Lincoln which had the same purpose, and there may have been others. Priests were appointed by the local government for a year at a time, and these

36.  Bronze figure of Jupiter from Huntingdonshire

12. The nine forts of the Saxon Shore,
from the Notitia Dignitatum

13. Painted wall plaster from Lullingstone villa, Kent

14. The Mildenhall silver dish

appointments were regarded as honours. Indeed, the priests received no salary; instead, they had to pay out of their own purses for the festivals held in the temples.

The spirit of the Emperor–god was linked with the four most important Roman gods in the heavens, Jupiter, Juno, Minerva and Mars. Jupiter (see plate 36), the most powerful of the gods, almost always had the names *Optimus Maximus* ('Best and Greatest') added, and these words are found on an altar from a fort in Cumberland, not far from Hadrian's Wall: 'To Jupiter Optimus Maximus, the First Cohort of Spaniards, which is commanded by Marcus Maenius Agrippa, tribune, set this up'. Juno was the wife of Jupiter and therefore queen of the gods; she was particularly responsible for women. And Minerva, the daughter of Jupiter, was in charge of all arts, crafts and skills, and therefore wisdom itself. Mars (see plate 37) was the god of war.

Many altars dedicated to the gods have been found in Britain, as well as small bronze and pottery figures of them. These figures stood in people's houses, in the household shrine, where the spirits of the family ancestors would be remembered. And along with these went whatever local gods might be worshipped (see plate 38). The Romans believed that every place had its own god or spirit, who looked over it and protected it in return for worship and sacrifice. The guardian spirit of a town, or a family, or indeed an individual person, was known as its genius; and along with this went a whole range of household gods, the lares, who looked after the house itself. So imagined figures of the genius and the lares stood alongside all the other gods. In Britain, the best of these have been found at Silchester.

The massacre of the Druids at their headquarters in Anglesey by Agricola and Suetonius, and the destruction of their holy places, did not mean that the old pre-Roman religion entirely vanished. The Druids were a menace to the Romans for political reasons, not religious ones, because these priests were leaders of resistance.

The memories and superstitions of the past survived in all sorts of local ways, though it is difficult now to sort out what was truly local and what truly Roman. Among the strangest of these old gods are the *Genii Cucullati*, the Cloaked Spirits, carvings of

37. Bronze figure of Mars from Forsdyke

38. Portable altar inscribed to local gods, from Vindolanda

whom have been found in several places in Britain, particularly along Hadrian's Wall but also in Lincoln and Gloucestershire. Most of these carvings show three hooded figures, with long cloaks. In some, the figures seem to be holding eggs, and it is thought that these may be symbols of immortality (see plate 39). A particularly mysterious carving, found near Cirencester, shows three such figures offering something – perhaps grapes – to a woman who is holding a large egg on her lap.

This woman may be a Mother-Goddess – another ancient spirit, who was shown in many carvings and figurines in pre-historic times all over the world. Many Roman inscriptions

39. Three cloaked spirits of Mother Goddesses from Lincoln

mentioning Mother-Goddesses have been found in Britain, most of them on monuments put up by soldiers from other parts of the Empire. One says: 'To the Mother-Goddesses of his native land Aurelius Juvenalis made this offering'. Another is dedicated 'To the Mother-Goddesses of all nations'. And one from Winchester is dedicated to the Mother-Goddesses of Italy, Germany, Gaul and Britain. What the soldiers who made these dedications may have felt is that the spirit of their native country was feminine, and that she gave birth to her people and looked after them like a real mother. At the same time, this Mother could be seen as the mysterious force behind all life and all growth, of crops and of the richness and fertility of the whole earth as well as the bearer of children.

Some of the cults that appeared in Roman Britain came from very far away. A jug excavated in London (see plate 40) carries the inscription *Londini Ad Fanum Isidis* – 'London, at the temple of Isis' – though no such temple has yet been found. Wherever it was, the ceremonies that went on there must have been to do with one

40. Inscribed jug from the temple of Isis

of the chief gods of the Egyptians, Isis, the wife of Osiris, whose worship went back thousands of years before the Romans. The Romans were fascinated by ancient Egyptian religion (the Roman historian Plutarch wrote an account of it), and there were probably some Roman followers of Egyptian rituals even before Egypt became a Roman province.

A much more widespread cult was that of Mithras, a god of the Zoroastrians in Persia. In the Roman Empire, including Britain, the worship of Mithras was particularly associated with soldiers, because it was a religion that demanded much courage and endurance. Worshippers had to pass through seven grades of initiation, though we know very little about what kinds of ritual these involved, because Mithraism was a deliberately mysterious faith and its secrets were closely guarded. We do know that the high point in the story of Mithras was his capture and killing of an enormous bull – a sacrifice by which he was supposed in some way to have saved the world (see plate 41).

41. Sculptured group representing Mithraic bull slaying, found in London

42. Altar of Mithras found at Carrawburgh

Mithras stabbing the bull is shown in many forms in the Roman world, in carvings and sculptures, mosaics and wall paintings. At Carrawburgh near Hadrian's Wall a Mithraeum, or temple of Mithras, has been found (see plate 42); but the most famous Mithraeum in Britain was found in London in 1954.

Among all the things discovered in this London temple, the most interesting were the sculptures (of Minerva and Mercury, as well as of Mithras and the bull) which had been deliberately hidden under the floor some time in the early fourth century A.D. Archaeologists think that the worshippers of Mithras were concealing them from Christians, who hated Mithraism so much because it seemed to be a horrible and wicked version of their own religion, with the 'sacrifice of salvation' involving the slaughter of a bull rather than the crucifixion of Jesus. In the year A.D. 312, the Emperor Constantine had made Christianity the official religion of the Roman Empire, replacing all other cults, and from

then on the worship of the Emperor, of Jupiter, and of all the other gods disappeared – in some places more slowly than others. But Christianity had already arrived in Britain at least a century before Constantine's decree. One of the earliest signs of this may be a scratched inscription found on the painted wall of a Roman house in Cirencester. The words are made into a square, which reads in one way ROTAS OPERA TENET AREPO SATOR – 'The sower Arepo guides the wheels at work'. This doesn't seem to make much sense – but read up and down and from side to side, they spell out another message in the form of a cross: PATER NOSTER, 'Our Father', the first words of the Lord's Prayer, with the letters A and O after them – that is, Alpha and Omega, the first and last letters of the Greek alphabet, the beginning and the end, which had quickly become a shorthand way of representing the Christian religion.

Perhaps the most moving of these very early Christian remains

```
              A
              P
              A
              T
              E
              R
A  PATERNOSTER  O
              O
              S
              T
              E
              R
              O
```

is an inscription found in a stone coffin at York. The coffin contained the skeleton of a woman, with her bracelets and armlets, ear-rings and mirror – and a tiny strip of bone, on which are the words SORORARE VIVAS IN DEO – 'Hail, sister, may you live in God'. It seems likely that this woman was buried at a time when Christianity was one of the few persecuted religions, before the official acceptance: the words seem almost secretly written.

With the adoption of Christianity, Christian signs and symbols occur in several parts of Roman Britain, and on many kinds of object: bowls, rings, spoons, lead water tanks (which may have had something to do with baptism), and in the villa at Lullingstone in Kent in a fourth-century room which was probably the chapel for the family that lived there. The *Chi-Rho* sign (the first letters in the Greek style of writing Christ's name, and another common shorthand way of representing the faith) is worked several times into the design of a wall painting here. And mosaic

pavements with Christian symbols have been found at two Roman villas in Dorset (Hinton St Mary and Frampton) and at Chedworth. Early in 1975, an amateur archaeologist came across the earliest hoard of Christian silver ever found, in a ploughed field at Water Newton, between Peterborough and Oundle. This was the site of the Roman town of Durobrivae. The hoard dates from the fourth century, and consists of nearly thirty silver objects – bowls, jugs, a two-handled cup, a large dish, a strainer, and a number of small triangular leaf-shaped plaques. Several of these things carry the Chi-Rho sign, and some have longer inscriptions.

Traces of only two definite churches of the Roman period

have been found, at Silchester and Caerwent. In a remote province like Britain, and particularly with a large army present which no doubt hung on to its old beliefs in private if not in public, Christianity probably spread more slowly than in parts of the Empire closer to Rome. Although Irish monks were coming into Britain and preaching by about the beginning of the fifth century A.D., it was to be years before the Christian religion took a firm hold in the country, in spite of official decrees from the Emperor in Rome. The 'conversion of England' came long after the Roman armies had left, when the buildings and roads of Roman Britain lay overgrown and in ruins.

# THE DECLINE AND FALL
## OF ROMAN BRITAIN

'Beyond the inhabited world' – that phrase by the Roman historian Dio Cassius, when he described the fear and gloom felt by the Roman Legions as they were about to embark for the invasion of Britain in A.D. 43, is not the way in which a third-century inhabitant of, say, London or Cirencester or Silchester would have felt about the province of Britannia; nor would the owner of one of the many prosperous villas. Although Britain was on the northern edge of the Empire, and although the presence of the army was always necessary to garrison and patrol the northern frontiers, large areas of the lowlands had become peaceful, settled, and as 'civilized' as most provinces; indeed, more civilized than some.

Yet in spite of its methodical organization and the way in which it managed to extend the same kind of life to many different kinds of province, the Roman Empire was not a changeless, static, solid piece of work. It had its economic troubles, sometimes local, sometimes general: bad harvests, inflation, difficulties in raising money for public works (such as road building and repair) which caused increased – and of course unpopular – taxation. There was the burden of paying for a large army. And off and on, and increasingly, there were hostile tribes and peoples to deal with, some from outside the Empire, some from within it, some from across the sea.

The Roman Empire was never easy or entirely peaceful along

its frontiers, whether in Germany or North Africa or in Britain itself. A few years before the building of Hadrian's Wall, there was a general native rising in the north; the forts built by Agricola in Scotland were overrun by the Caledonian tribes, and further south the Brigantes rebelled and destroyed the Ninth Legion which was stationed at York. Although the Emperors Hadrian and Antoninus Pius pushed the frontier back again and built their great walls, the Brigantes rose in A.D. 154–155, and caused trouble as far south as Derbyshire. Twenty-five years later, a series of rebellions and invasions from the north began which went on for the next quarter of a century. Matters were made worse by a mutiny among some army units in Britain, and by a struggle between three military leaders to become Emperor. All this was temporarily settled by the Emperor Septimius Severus, who managed to rebuild Hadrian's Wall (the Antonine Wall was abandoned) and to strike as far north as Aberdeenshire in Scotland. For almost a century, the island was comparatively quiet.

Towards the end of Severus's reign (he died on one of his visits to Britain, at York in the year 211), the island was divided into two provinces, Britannia Superior and Britannia Inferior – that is, Upper Britain and Lower Britain. There were separate governors, and the idea may have been to split the army in two so that no single man would have control over all the Legions and auxiliaries. More and more it was army officers who made and unmade Emperors, and an army unified under one commander was seen to have dangers.

By the year 280 or so, there were signs of new trouble. Not only did the northern tribes again manage to drive the troops from Hadrian's Wall, but groups of raiders from what are now the borders of Denmark and Germany began to attack the coasts of both Gaul and Britain. These were the Saxons and the Franks, and it was the Saxons in particular who in the end were going to shape the future of Britain. At first they were chiefly sea pirates grabbing what they could from cargo ships in the North Sea and the Channel. Then they started their raids on the coasts themselves, looting and killing. One of the signs of the uncertainty such raids brought to the coastal inhabitants of southern and eastern

Britain is the number of coin hoards dating from this period which have been found there – five of them near Eastbourne in Sussex, for example. The Romano-British settlers who buried these coins hoped, no doubt, that the money would be safe from the raiders. So it was – but the settlers evidently never managed to recover it. Perhaps they were killed, or perhaps they hurriedly moved inland and never came back.

Things became so bad that a special naval force was created to try to keep the seas clear of pirates from Belgium to Brittany. This was the Classis Britannica (the British Fleet); and the man who was put in charge of it, Carausius (see plate 43), was an experienced Roman naval officer whose people came from the borders of Gaul and Germany, but who had settled in what is now Holland. In the year 284, Carausius was commanded by the Emperor Diocletian to make the seas safe. His headquarters were at Boulogne, in Gaul.

43. Carausius

For two years, Carausius held this job. But in A.D. 286, Diocletian decided to share his imperial throne with a general, Maximian, and one of the first things Maximian did was to dismiss Carausius from the command of the Channel Fleet and order him to come to Rome. We know about this only from the 'official' Roman historians, but at any rate their version of what had happened was that Carausius, far from stopping the Saxon and Frankish raiders from attacking the coasts of both Britain and Gaul, had allowed them to get away with the loot and had then boarded their ships at sea and had kept the treasures for himself. And when Maximian summoned him to Rome, Carausius – and all his fleet – revolted. Carausius declared himself Emperor – not of the whole Roman Empire, but of the areas his fleet controlled: part of Gaul, parts of what are now Belgium and Holland, and the whole of Britain.

Carausius managed to rule this small empire of his for seven years. A naval force that Maximian sent to fight him was either lost at sea because of bad weather or was defeated by Carausius. After his 'unilateral declaration of independence', Carausius had large numbers of coins minted carrying his name and the title of Emperor. He had the loyalty of the three Legions stationed in Britain at the time, and that of the army units in Boulogne. He even managed to have his Empire 'recognized' by the central government in Rome – though he must have realized that his days were numbered. Although the central government was weaker than it had been, with so many tribes on the frontiers causing trouble and stretching the Roman armies almost to breaking point, it was not likely to tolerate a usurper of Carausius's sort for long.

At this period there is some very solid evidence along the southern and eastern coasts, but it is evidence about which archaeologists disagree. From Brancaster, on the north coast of Norfolk, down to Portchester, on the coast of Hampshire near Portsmouth, there is a series of nine stone forts. These are known as the 'Saxon Shore' forts (see colour plate 12). Some of them, though of course in ruins, are still very impressive, especially those at Burgh Castle, near Yarmouth in Norfolk (see plate 44), Richborough in Kent, and Portchester. Most of them were built at the end of the third century, though a few existed in much smaller form before that. For years, modern archaeologists accepted the idea that their reconstruction and expansion in the late third century was in order to make them defences against the Saxon pirates; and certainly this is how they were meant to be used when a new official, with the splended title of *Comes Litoris Saxonici* (Count of the Saxon Shore), was appointed at the beginning of the fourth century. But a more recent theory is that, far from being a defence against the Saxons, they were first intended to be Carausius's bulwark against the fleet which the central government in Rome was bound to send to attack him.

44. The south-east angle tower and south wall of Burgh Castle, Norfolk

Whichever is the true explanation, the separate 'empire' of Carausius was doomed. In A.D. 294, he was murdered by Allectus, one of his chief officers, who wanted to be Emperor himself; and two years later a Roman army captured Boulogne and a Roman fleet sailed from there to the south coast, near the Isle of Wight. Landing there, the Imperial Army met the army of Allectus, probably in north-east Hampshire, and defeated it. While this was going on, the northern tribes again poured in, destroying parts of Chester and York; Allectus in his desperation had pulled out too many soldiers from the north to the south, and the frontiers had not been properly defended. The breakaway empire was finished.

For a second time Britain was under the central rule of Rome, for another 125 years. But now the Saxons and Franks began to unite with the northern tribes, the Picts and the Scots, and together these fierce anti-Roman forces played havoc with the province. More and more Roman troops had been withdrawn to deal with revolts and raids on the continent of Europe. The Emperor Constantine I (the one who had officially made Christianity the religion of the Empire) was a strong and decisive ruler, and during his reign (306–330) Britain managed to recover, at least in its lowland areas, some of its prosperity; during these twenty-five years or so there are signs of rebuilding and improvement both in the towns and in the villas. But it was just a peaceful lull before the final onslaught of storms. After the death of Constantine, within a few years a Romano-British military leader called Magnentius briefly took over as usurper in both Britain and Gaul: the only difference was that, unlike Carausius, he was a native of Britain. To the tribes who skirmished round the shores, there was no difference; nor was there any to the Picts and Scots to the north.

From now on, there is a confusing picture of generals from the central government (such as Theodosius) trying to make order in Britain, conflicting with usurpers (such as the general Maximus, a Spaniard who had commanded the troops in Britain and had then declared himself Emperor), and both struggling to keep the invading tribes at bay. It was a chaotic situation. By the year

409, the Romano-Britains were sending appeals to the Emperor Honorius (see plate 45) to help them withstand the assaults of the Franks and Saxons, to whom by now had been added the Angles, another group of tribes from northern Germany. But the centre of the Empire was in such a confused state that Honorius could do nothing for them. In the year 410, Rome itself was sacked by the Goths, and the Legions were withdrawn from Britain. The message was that the population would have to fend for itself as best it could.

45. Honorius

In all these pirate raids, invasions, usurping generals and brief periods of peace, it is difficult to find out what life for people in Britain was like. In the north and along the eastern and southern coasts, it must have been an almost constant business of flight and return, defence and survival. Not only did the settlers bury hoards of coins, they hid away other treasure too. The most famous example is the Mildenhall Treasure: this was a vast collection of silver plates and other dishes, buried by a rich Roman family in an attempt to save it from Saxon raiders, some time in the fourth or fifth century A.D. It was ploughed up by chance in 1942, near the small town of Mildenhall in Suffolk. The largest dish weighs 18 lbs and measures two feet across (see colour plate 14).

By the beginning of the fifth century, the Saxons were not only raiding, they were settling in East Anglia and in the East Riding of Yorkshire: their pottery has been found there, and not just the pottery they brought with them but pieces that had obviously been made in Romano-British kilns but adapted in style to their own taste. Very early Saxon cemeteries have been found in these areas, showing that they lived and died there.

It was a return, in a way, to the time almost four hundred years earlier, before the invasion of Claudius. But only in a way: the main difference was that now the settled population of Britain was much larger, and that it thought of itself as Roman. Two centuries earlier – so far back in time that the inhabitants of Britain must have thought it a decree that lasted from the beginning – the Emperor in Rome had granted full citizenship of the Empire to every free-born subject. The shopkeeper in Corinium, the glass manufacturer in Venta Icenorum, the magistrate in Verulamium, the villa owner of Chedworth, the army officer who had retired and was running a farm somewhere in Lincolnshire – all of them were Roman citizens, brought up in the ways of the Empire, accustomed to its laws, fond of their imperial pleasures in public baths, amphitheatres, imported wines, imported household decorations. They were born and bred in Britain (except probably for the army officer – and even he had chosen to stay in the country where he had done his military service); but they also belonged to Rome, to its ways and traditions. And now all of that was in peril.

In these confused last years of Romano-British life, it seems that the inhabitants even went to the desperate lengths of hiring European mercenaries (people who were willing to fight for anyone so long as they were paid), and at least some of these mercenaries were themselves from the enemy lands of the Angles and Saxons. Just outside the east gate of Venta Icenorum in Norfolk, a large Anglo-Saxon cemetery was found, and some of the pottery in it (containing cremations) has been dated by archaeologists to the years just before A.D. 400. Hired to defend the town dwellers against attack by Anglo-Saxon fellow-countrymen, they can hardly have been a very reliable force.

Who ruled Britain? Neither the central government in Rome nor Britain itself regarded the province as having finally been lost: appeals for help were being made to Rome at least as late as A.D. 446, and, though no such help came, it is thought that for years Rome intended to restore its rule to the island. The Roman historian Procopius, writing a century later, says that after the death of the Emperor Constantine III in the year 411, Britain was ruled by tyrannoi – not tyrants, but usurpers. But in this case they would not be usurpers like Carausius, defying the Roman Empire; instead, they were local Romano-British military leaders, many of them probably trained in the Roman army, who tried to resist the invaders from the north, south and east. Yet gradually they were overwhelmed.

One by one the towns were deserted, and their inhabitants (those who were not killed by the Angles and Saxons, or made into slaves) moved away – some to Gaul, but most to Wales. In early Welsh literature, there is mention of these people and of their military leaders, who were called Gwledig in Welsh ('commanders') and who were said to wear Roman military insignia. The villas and farms were abandoned, their fields quickly becoming overgrown. All over lowland Britain, archaeologists have found the signs of collapsed walls and roofs from this period, fire and hasty burials. As the generations followed, Latin was gradually forgotten, with Anglo-Saxon taking over in the lowlands and the Celtic language asserting itself (for the Celts had never been totally suppressed) in the highlands of the west and north. Even now, some Latin words survive in Welsh, as 'borrowings' from the Romano-British who found refuge in Wales: for example, the Welsh word *ffenestr* comes from the Latin *fenestra* (window).

The Anglo-Saxons were not town dwellers; the small village, with its open fields round it, was their natural place. Nor would they have felt at home in the villas, which must have seemed as foreign to them as the neat and identical farmhouses of the Italian colonial settlers in Libya did in modern times to the Arab tribesmen. The Roman drainage ditches and canals of the Fens flooded and silted up; the miles and miles of Roman roads grew high with weeds and grass, like disused railway lines. Most useless of all were the great public buildings – the basilicas, the temples, the bath-houses – and the military installations. Both Walls in the north were derelict by now, and the forts of the Saxon Shore, and the garrison centres at York, Chester and Caerleon.

It was the Roman towns in the west that managed to survive longest, since they were furthest away from the early Anglo-Saxon settlements. Cirencester, for example, seems to have had some kind of organized life well into the fifth century, with the town defences being repaired and markets being held in the forum. But even here there are signs of the roads becoming choked with mud and overgrown, and of unburied skeletons lying where the bodies had fallen – perhaps dying of plague rather than being killed by invaders, for in the middle of the fifth century a great plague spread across Europe from the east and maybe reached Britain. Yet the west of Britain, too, was to fall to the Anglo-Saxons. The *Anglo-Saxon Chronicle* records that in A.D. 577

> Cuthwine and Ceawlin fought against the Britons and killed three kings, Conmail, Condidan and Farinmail, at the place which is called Dyrham. And they captured three of their cities, Gloucester, Cirencester and Bath.

Bath, a Roman city almost wholly devoted to the very Roman pleasures of the baths themselves, must have seemed the strangest place of all to the Anglo-Saxons when they captured it. Years later, when Britain was still inhabited by Saxons but no doubt long after any clear memory survived of who the Romans were or what they had done, an Anglo-Saxon poet wrote of some 'works of giants' which he had seen in ruins. He was certainly describing the ruins of some Roman city, and the details towards the end seem to suggest that it may have been Bath. The manuscript is damaged, so that not all of it can be read, but enough is there to show the wonder – and the sadness – of the poet as he contemplated the decay of time.

> Splendid this rampart is, though fate destroyed it,
> The city buildings fell apart, the works
> Of giants crumble. Tumbled are the towers,
> Ruined the roofs, and broken the barred gate,
> Frost in the plaster, all the ceilings gape,
> Torn and collapsed and eaten up by age.
> And grit holds in its grip, the hard embrace
> Of earth, the dead departed master-builders,
> Until a hundred generations now
> Of people have passed by. Often this wall

Stained red and grey with lichen has stood by
Surviving storms while kingdoms rose and fell.
And now the high curved wall itself has fallen. . .
Resolute masons, skilled in rounded building
Wondrously linked the framework with iron bonds.
The public halls were bright, with lofty gables,
Bath-houses many; great the cheerful noise
And many mead-halls filled with human pleasures,
Till mighty fate brought change upon it all.
Slaughter was widespread, pestilence was rife,
And death took all those valiant men away.
The martial halls became deserted places,
The city crumbled, its repairers fell,
Its armies to the earth. And so these halls
Are empty, and this red curved roof now sheds
Its tiles, decay has brought it to the ground,
Smashed it to piles of rubble, where long since
A host of heroes, glorious, gold-adorned,
Gleaming in splendour, proud and flushed with wine,
Shone in their armour, gazed on gems and treasure,
On silver, riches, wealth and jewellery,
On this bright city with its wide domains.
Stone buildings stood, and the hot stream cast forth
Wide sprays of water, which a wall enclosed
In its bright compass, where convenient
Stood hot baths ready for them at the centre.
Hot streams poured forth over the clear grey stone,
To the round pool and down into the baths. . . .

🔲🔲🔲🔲🔲

# POSTSCRIPT

🔲🔲🔲🔲🔲

THE gradual collapse of not only Roman Britain but of the whole Roman Empire is one of the greatest and saddest stories in human history. For all their faults, the Romans had managed to bring peace, good government, a sense of order and a sense of civilization to a large part of the western world. The unity and the uniformity of the Empire allowed it both to adapt to whatever local features seemed worthwhile, and, even after its passing, to hand on a legacy many parts of which still survive, large and small. There is the high proportion of Latin words (estimated at about one-third) in the English language, as well as the whole foundation of French, Italian, Spanish and Portuguese. There is the idea of law; and Roman law is still the basis of many codes of justice. There is our alphabet; and we still use Roman numerals for some purposes, and Roman calendar names for some of our months. In building, the Romans were pioneers in making roads, in manufacturing brick and concrete, in the construction of the arch for bridges, domes and vaults, in drainage and sewer systems, in central heating. As far as western civilization is concerned, the Romans invented banking and the public postal system. There is the whole heritage of Latin literature: Virgil, Ovid, Lucretius, Catullus, Juvenal, Martial, Seneca, and dozens of other poets and writers, as well as the historians and political writers, such as Cicero. And it was through the channels of the Roman Empire that Christianity spread.

The poet Thomas Hardy, visiting Italy in April 1887, went to the ruins of the Roman theatre at Fiesole, just outside Florence;

and he wrote a poem about a particular incident that happened to him there which made him realize how far the Roman Empire spread. Hardy lived near Dorchester in Dorset – the Roman town of Durnovaria; and here he was, in 1887, hundreds and hundreds of miles away from his home.

> I traced the Circus whose gray stones incline
> Where Rome and dim Etruria interjoin,
> Till came a child who showed an ancient coin
> That bore the image of a Constantine.
> She lightly passed; nor did she once opine
> How, better than all books, she had raised for me
> In swift perspective Europe's history
> Through the vast years of Caesar's sceptred line.
>
> For in my distant plot of English loam
> 'Twas but to delve, and straightway there to find
> Coins of like impress. As with one half blind
> Whom common simples cure, her act flashed home
> In that mute moment to my opened mind
> The power, the pride, the reach of perished Rome.

ഞ്ഞ്ഞ്ഞ്ഞ്ഞ്

# BIBLIOGRAPHY

ഞ്ഞ്ഞ്ഞ്ഞ്ഞ്

### I. SOURCE MATERIAL

Birley, A. *Life in Roman Britain*. Batsford, London, 1964

Birley, R. *Discoveries at Vindolanda*. Frank Graham, Newcastle, 1973

*Guide to the Antiquities of Roman Britain*. British Museum, London, 1971

Clarke, J. and D. *Camulodunum*. Ginn, London, 1971

Clarke, R. Rainbird. *East Anglia*. Thames and Hudson, London, 1960

Collingwood, R. G. and Richmond, I. *The Archaeology of Roman Britain*. Methuen, London, 1969

Cottrell, L. *The Roman Forts of the Saxon Shore*. H.M.S.O., London, 1971

Cunliffe, Barry. *Roman Bath Discovered*. Routledge and Kegan Paul, London, 1971

Cunliffe, Barry. *Fishbourne: A Roman Palace and its Garden*. Thames and Hudson, London, 1971.

Frere, S. *Britannia*. Routledge and Kegan Paul, London, 1967

Grimes, W. F. *The Excavation of Roman and Medieval London*. Routledge and Kegan Paul, London, 1968

Liversidge, J. *Britain in the Roman Empire*. Routledge and Kegan Paul, London, 1968

Margary, I. D. *Roman Roads in Britain*. John Baker, London, 1973

McWhirr, A. *Verulamium*. Ginn, London, 1971

Merrifield, R. *The Roman City of London*. Benn, London, 1965

Quennell, M. and C. H. B. *Everyday Life in Roman Britain*. Batsford, London, 1952

Richmond, I. A. *Roman Britain*. Penguin, Harmondsworth, 1955

Wacher, J. *Corinium*. Ginn, London, 1971

Webster, G. and Dudley, D. R. *The Roman Conquest of Britain*, Pan, London, 1973

Wilson, Roger J. A. *A Guide to Roman Remains in Britain*. Constable, London, 1975

Young, H. W. *Roman London*. H.M.S.O., London, 1962

## 2. SOURCE MATERIAL IN TRANSLATION

Caesar, Julius. *The Gallic Wars and Other Commentaries*. Translated by W. A. MacDevitt, with an introduction by Thomas de Quincey. Dent, London, 1939

Tacitus. *Agricola and Germania*. Translated by H. Mattingley. Penguin, Harmondsworth, 1970

## 3. NON-FICTION FOR THE SAME AGE GROUP

Cunliffe, Barry. *Rome and the Barbarians*. Bodley Head, London, 1975

Grant, Michael. *The Roman Forum*. Weidenfeld and Nicolson, London, 1970

Jones, David. *Your Book of Roman Britain*. Faber and Faber, London, 1973

Leacroft, H. and R. *Buildings of Ancient Rome*. Brockhampton, Leicester, 1969

## 4. FICTION FOR THE SAME AGE GROUP

Dillon, Eilis. *Living in Imperial Rome*. Faber and Faber, London, 1974

Goscinny and Uderzo. *Asterix in Britain*. Brockhampton, Leicester, 1970

Graves, Robert. *Claudius the God*. Penguin, Harmondsworth, 1969

Graves, Robert. *I Claudius*. Penguin, Harmondsworth, 1969

Kipling, Rudyard. *Puck of Pook's Hill*. Macmillan, London, 1965

Macaulay, David. *City*. Collins, London, 1975

Mitchison, Naomi. *The Conquered*. Jonathan Cape, London, 1923

Ray, Mary. *The Ides of March*. Faber and Faber, London, 1974

Ray, Mary. *Spring Tide*. Faber and Faber, London, 1969

Scott, John. *The Provincial Governor*. Longmans, London, 1971

Seton, Anya. *The Mistletoe and the Sword*. Coronet, London, 1974

Sutcliff, Rosemary. *The Eagle of the Ninth*. Oxford University Press, Oxford, 1970

Sutcliff, Rosemary. *The Lantern Bearers*. Oxford University Press, Oxford, 1959

Sutcliff, Rosemary. *The Mark of the Horse Lord*. Oxford University Press, Oxford, 1965

Sutcliff, Rosemary. *The Silver Branch*. Oxford University Press, Oxford, 1957

Trease, Geoffrey. *Word to Caesar*. Macmillam, London, 1958

Treece, Henry. *The Eagles Have Flown*. Bodley Head, London, 1954

Treece, Henry. *Legions of the Eagle*. Bodley Head, London, 1954